To Life!

High Holy Day

Prayer Book

Rosh HaShanah / Yom Kippur

מחזור לחיים

ראש השנה / יום כפור

Edited and Compiled by Rabbi Shafir Lobb

DEDICATION

In loving memory of my parents,

Rabbi Sholom and Marion Silver

And my husband's parents,

George and Catherine Lobb

And with special love to the man who accompanies me on my journey,

William Lobb

TABLE OF CONTENTS

ACKNOWLEDGMENTS AND INTRODUCTION

Welcome to the To Life! High Holy Day Prayer Book. The Hebrew word for a High Holy Day Prayer Book is *Machzor*, which means cycle. The High Holy Days mark another year on the Hebrew Calendar and so a cycle is completed. Once again, it is time for us to make a spiritual accounting between ourselves and our loved ones and our communities and the Holy One, the innermost Source of Life.

This is a special edition *Machzor* for use in Assisted Living and other care facilities. It is a combined edition for Rosh Hashanah and Yom Kippur, combining *To Life! High Holy Day Prayer Book - Rosh HaShanah* and *To Life! High Holy Day Prayer Book – Yom Kippur* into a single volume. It supports a 30 minute - 1 hour Rosh HaShanah service and a 30 minute - 1 hour Yom Kippur service (or multiple short Yom Kippur services, such as Kol Nidrei, Yizkor, etc) with large font Hebrew, transliteration and translation. Special attention was given to meaningful wording for the residents and guests of these facilities. Enough variety of liturgy is presented to allow the leader to fashion a particular service according to individual tastes and the requirements of the facility. A particular service might feel more in one denomination or across denominations depending on how the particular service is crafted. In general, seating instructions call for sitting as much as possible and always allow for sitting when the individual would be more comfortable sitting (specific wording addresses sitting on each page where the congregation is standing.)

Rabbi Shafir Lobb, who authored, edited and compiled the original of this *machzor*, strove to combine English prayers and readings with the current liturgy and popular liturgical songs to help those who join in the journey of these Holy Days find the words and songs that will help them with their Soul Work. This English pagination edition is produced by special permission of Judaic Press, who retains rights to all other editions not released through CreateSpace ISBNs.

Efforts were made to use clear and large fonts, both for Hebrew and English. All Hebrew liturgy is translated using Times New Roman if the translation is not part of the liturgy read aloud or Book Antiqua if it is used as a reading or song. Transliteration of all of the Hebrew liturgy (to allow non-Hebrew readers to join in with the Hebrew liturgy) that is normally read aloud, chanted or sung is done using Arial, with the accented syllable in **bold**. We follow the convention that what the reader reads alone is in regular font and what the congregation reads in unison (whether responsive or not) is in *italics*.

Particular effort was made to make the Torah Readings more accessible. Each verse is transliterated and translated. Rabbi Lobb did the English translations that are used throughout the book, including the Torah readings. The Torah reading for Rosh HaShanah was shortened to two short (3+) *aliyot* featuring the first verses and the climax of the raised knife and angel appearance. The reading of the *Akeda*, the Binding, was selected over the story of the divorce of Hagar to align with Reform convention and also as a recognition that in the care facility setting, celebration of Rosh HaShanah is likely to be only one day. The Torah reading for Yom Kippur was shortened to six *pasukim* (16:29-34), allowing for one *aliyah* or two short (3+) *aliyot*. There is no haftarah included for Rosh HaShanah; a customized rendering of Jonah (abbreviated and with loyal excerpts) is included in Yom Kippur without blessings

The Yizkor service includes one general version of the Yizkor prayers for male and female rather than the traditional inclusion of many different versions for specific relationships to the worshipper. Powerful English readings are included in this short service. There is a section titled YIZKOR RITUAL which can also serve as a moment of silence or similar use by the leader and it concludes with the Yizkor prayers.

A single combined Rosh HaShanah / Yom Kippur service can also be crafted using the liturgy repeated in both services only once as a combined service and then selecting the desired readings between these key elements. While there are significant differences in the liturgy and tone of the two holidays, the basic liturgy is shared. A unique segment for Rosh HaShanah is the Shofar Service and for Yom Kippur the unique segments include Kol Nidre, *Ashamnu* and the *Al Cheit* prayers, Yizkor and Ne'ila. Similar elements include the Shema and her blessings, the *Amidah* (*tefilah*), *Unetane Tokef* and a Torah Service (although the readings are naturally quite different.)

All non-attributed original text is the work of Rabbi Shafir Lobb. Song lyrics are attributed to the artists in the body of the *machzor*. We thank the many artists who contributed artwork, including those whose artwork is unsigned and/or on the public domain. Special thanks go to Rabbi Ayla Grafstein, Carol S. Kestler, Bill Lobb, Rabbi Shafir Lobb, Rabbi Marcia Prager, Ann Syl, and others whose names have become detached from their work through the Public Domain, but whose effort and vision is appreciated. In cases where there are copyrights, all rights remain with the artist for any use other than this prayer book.

Rabbi Shafir Lobb maintains any and all rights to her work for any use other than this prayer book. Rabbi Lobb also acknowledges and holds responsibility for any and all errors remaining in this *machzor*. When you find one, please alert her at rebshafir@earthlink.net so that it might be corrected in future printings or editions.

Thank You to the compilers of other *Machzorim* and *Siddurim* whose work served as idea-seed and inspiration and guidance: Rabbi Ayla Grafstein (Ruach Hamidbar); Rabbi Marcia Prager (P'nai Or - Philadelphia), Rabbi Daniel Siegel (Siddur Kol Koreh), Rabbi

Joe Weizenbaum (Ner Tamid), Rabbi David Zaslow (Ivdu et Hashem b'Simcha), and Rabbis Allen S. Maller, Jeffrey A. Marx, Richard Schachet, z"l and Jerry Fisher (Tikunay Nefashot - Spiritual Renewal). A very special thank you goes to Rabbi Daniel Siegel for his many, many hours of proofing the Hebrew and its transliteration as well as making wonderful suggestions for improving the overall prayer book.

A special thank you also goes to Rabbis Zalman Shachter-Shalomi, Marcia Prager, Daniel Siegel, Shaya Isenberg, Elliot Ginsburg and Shefa Gold. Their teaching and guidance is an intrinsic part of this book. Without them, it would not have happened.

Thanks beyond measure go to William Lobb, whose love, support and technical expertise are beyond measure. Without him, this project would not have been completed. Without him, my computer would be a pile of rubble wherever it might have landed and I would probably be bald by now.

If you know of any work that has been misattributed or is unattributed and you know the correct artist/author, please advise us at rebshafir@earthlink.net.

Thank you for using this prayer book for your High Holy Day journey and for taking the time and interest to read this introduction.

L'Shanah Tovah Tikateivu uGmar Chatima Tovah (May you be inscribed and sealed into the Book of Life for a good year!)

5772 / 2011

Rosh HaShanah Service

בְּרֹאשׁ הַשָּׁנָה יִכָּתֵבוּן, וּבְיוֹם צוֹם כִּפּוּר יֵחָתֵמוּן.

BeRosh HaShanah yikateivun. Uv'Yom Tzom Kippur yeichateimun.

On Rosh Hashanah it is written And on Yom Kippur it is sealed:

Rosh HaShanah Service

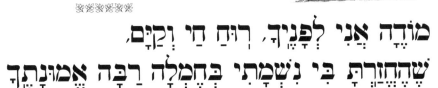

מוֹדָה אֲנִי לְפָנֶיךָ, רוּחַ חַי וְקַיָּם,
שֶׁהֶחֱזַרְתָּ בִּי נִשְׁמָתִי בְּחֶמְלָה רַבָּה אֱמוּנָתֶךָ

Modah/**deh** ani lifa**ne**cha, **ru**-ach chai veka**yam**,
shecha**zar**ta biy nishmati bechem**la** ra**bah** emunatecha.

I gratefully acknowledge the face of God; Spirit lives and endures; You return my soul
to me with compassion; How great is your faith in me. (R. Shefa Gold)

מַה טֹּבוּ אֹהָלֶיךָ יַעֲקֹב, מִשְׁכְּנֹתֶיךָ יִשְׂרָאֵל.

Mah **to**vu oha**le**cha Ya-a**kov**, Mishkeno**te**cha Yisra-**eil**.
Blessings flow into the world from the Source of Life.
Be a vessel for the lovesong of God © R. Hanna Tiferet Siegel
How good are your tents, Ya-akov, your indwelling places, Israel.

Awaken arise to the wholeness of your being
Awaken arise to the beauty of your soul (2x)

הִתְעוֹרְרִי הִתְעוֹרְרִי. כִּי בָא אוֹרֵךְ קוּמִי אוֹרִי.

Hit'ore**ri** hit'ore**ri** ki va **o**rech, **Ku**mi ori
© R. Hanna Tiferet Siegel

אֱלֹהַי נְשָׁמָה שֶׁנָּתַתָּ בִּי טְהוֹרָה הִיא.

Elo**hai** n'sha**mah** shena**ta**ta bi teho**rah** hi.
My God, the life and soul which You placed within me are pure.

מַה גָּדְלוּ מַעֲשֶׂיךָ יהוה מְאֹד עָמְקוּ מַחְשְׁבֹתֶיךָ. הַלְלוּיָהּ.

Ma gad**lu** ma-a**se**cha Yah me-**od** am**ku** machshevo**te**cha. (Hallelu**Yahh**)
How great are Your actions, Adonai; Your thoughts are very deep. (HalleluYah - Praise God)

בָּרוּךְ שֶׁאָמַר, בְּרוּכָה שֶׁאָמְרָה, וְהָיָה הָעוֹלָם.

Ba**ruch** she-**amar**, Bru**chah** she-am**rah** v'ha**yah** ha-**olam**.
Blessed is He, Blessed is She, Blessed are We who speak and are heard.
© R. Hanna Tiferet Siegel

Nish-ma-**ti** a-hu-**vah** le-hit-cha-**reit** ha-kli-**pah**
le-tshu-**vah** u-sli-**chah**
le-to-**dah** u-vra-**chah** Halelluh**Yahh**, Halelluh**Yahh**

נִשְׁמָתִי אָהוּבָה
לְהִתְחָרֵט הַקְּלִיפָּה
לִתְשׁוּבָה וּסְלִיחָה
לְתוֹדָה וּבְרָכָה
הַלְלוּיָהּ הַלְלוּיָהּ

O my Soul, I Love You,
Pain and Sorrow from my life, Repenting and Releasing
Thanks to You, Blessings come
HalelluhYahh   HalelluhYahh

Merciful One,
Today celebrates the first day of the new year.
From this perspective, last year was rough, some of it
horrific, and yet, some of it wondrous and beautiful.
Today brings not only the promise of a new day,
it brings the promise of a new year,
a whole year gone and an entirely new one
on which to make our mark.

> *God, help us to move bravely and courageously into the new year.*
> *Please help us make it a year of doing the things we need to do*
> *while making sure we take care of this planet and all of its inhabitants.*

And through our doing, may we feel Your Presence through the joy and support
of community and friends.
May we come to know that Your Presence is
always there for us.
It is we who need to open our hearts and souls
to Your Presence through being present.

> *Dear One, help us to return to You,*
> *and return to who we truly are.*

Thank You, God of us all, for the gift of this new year.

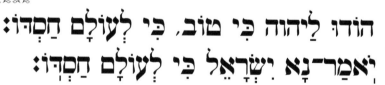

הוֹדוּ לַיהוה כִּי טוֹב, כִּי לְעוֹלָם חַסְדּוֹ:
יֹאמַר־נָא יִשְׂרָאֵל כִּי לְעוֹלָם חַסְדּוֹ:

Ho**du** la'Ado**nai** ki tov, ki l'**olam** chas**do**:
Yomar na Yisra-**eil**, ki l'**olam** chas**do**:
Let all who revere God's Name now say, "Ki l'olam chasdo"
Sing praise to the One for God is good, ki l'olam chasdo.

Give thanks to Adonai for God is good and God's mercy endures forever.
Say it, please, Israel for God's mercy endures forever. Ps 118:1-2

הִנֵּה מַה טּוֹב וּמַה נָּעִים שֶׁבֶת אַחִים גַּם יָחַד.

Hi**nei** ma tov u**mah** na-**iym** she**vet** a**chiym** gam ya**chad**.

Behold how good and how pleasant it is when brethren dwell together.

הַלְלוּהוּ בְּצִלְצְלֵי שָׁמַע, הַלְלוּהוּ בְּצִלְצְלֵי תְרוּעָה: כֹּל הַנְּשָׁמָה תְּהַלֵּל יָהּ הַלְלוּיָהּ.

Hale**lu**hu betziltze**lei sha**ma. Hale**lu**hu betziltze**lei** tru'**ah**.
Kol hansha**mah** teha**leil** Yahh, Halelu**Yahh**.

Praise the Source with crashing cymbals! Praise the Source with resounding voice!
Let all who breathe now praise their Source! Hallelujah (Praise Yahh)! (Psalm 150)

God, the time has come again for me to do the hardest work I can do,
working on my Self. I need Your help if I am to be able to do it well.

Help me face questions I wish to avoid!
Help me accept truths which do not comfort!
I wish to journey to the light, but the path is hidden
by all of the promises I never kept, by the goodness I forgot.

The gates of prayer are sometimes open and sometimes closed,
while the gates of repentance are always open.
The Holy One's hand is always open to receive penitents.
When we see You wield Your power with love and compassion,
it becomes easier to reach out our hands to You.

There is no sadder confession than
"I know I am doing wrong, but it is too late now to change."
This is to surrender to despair.
Rosh HaShanah comes with a great gift --
the opportunity to begin again.
Not one of us has sunk so low that we cannot rise up.

The old year is gone. The ledger is closed.
Our Book of Life is now open
to a new page, a page bright with whiteness.
No sins blot it, no indiscretions blemish it.

Slowly the invisible pen begins to record our life;
and it is given to us to direct the pen.

It becomes ever harder to write clear and fine words and phrases.
And yet, we are invited to try and are challenged to succeed.

On Rosh HaShanah, we receive the gift of beginning again.
We know now what we did not know then.
What will we do with this knowledge?
How will we use this gift?

❀❀❀❀❀

נִשְׁמַת כָּל חַי, תְּבָרֵךְ אֶת שִׁמְךָ יהוה אֱלֹהֵינוּ.

Nish**mat** kol chai, teva**reich** et shim**cha** (Yahh or Ado**nai**) Elo**hei**nu.
The breath of all life, Praises You, (Yahh or Adonai) our God.

❀❀❀❀❀

Sho**chein**, sho**chein** ad
Ma**rom** veka**dosh** Shemo
vecha**tuv**, ka**dosh** Shemo...
Sho**chein**...

שׁוֹכֵן שׁוֹכֵן עַד,
מָרוֹם וְקָדוֹשׁ שְׁמוֹ:
וְכָתוּב, קָדוֹשׁ שְׁמוֹ ...... שׁוֹכֵן...

You dwell within, for all time
Exalted, sacred are You
It is written, Sacred are You... Sho**chein**...

The righteous rejoice in You
The upright seek Your glory
It is written, Sacred are You... Sho**chein**...

❀❀❀❀❀

CHATZI KADDISH   חצי קדיש

יִתְגַּדַּל וְיִתְקַדַּשׁ שְׁמֵהּ רַבָּא. בְּעָלְמָא דִּי בְרָא כִרְעוּתֵהּ,
וְיַמְלִיךְ מַלְכוּתֵהּ בְּחַיֵּיכוֹן וּבְיוֹמֵיכוֹן וּבְחַיֵּי דְכָל בֵּית יִשְׂרָאֵל.
בַּעֲגָלָא וּבִזְמַן קָרִיב וְאִמְרוּ אָמֵן:

יְהֵא שְׁמֵהּ רַבָּא מְבָרַךְ לְעָלַם וּלְעָלְמֵי עָלְמַיָּא:

יִתְבָּרַךְ וְיִשְׁתַּבַּח, וְיִתְפָּאַר וְיִתְרוֹמַם וְיִתְנַשֵּׂא וְיִתְהַדָּר וְיִתְעַלֶּה
וְיִתְהַלָּל שְׁמֵהּ דְּקֻדְשָׁא בְּרִיךְ הוּא לְעֵלָּא לְעֵלָּא מִכָּל בִּרְכָתָא
וְשִׁירָתָא, תֻּשְׁבְּחָתָא וְנֶחֱמָתָא, דַּאֲמִירָן בְּעָלְמָא, וְאִמְרוּ אָמֵן:

Yitga**dal** v'yitka**dash** shi**mei** ra**ba**. B'al**ma** di vera chiru**tei**, veyam**lich** malchu**tei**
bechayei**chon** uv'yomei**chon** uv'cha**yei** de**chol** beit Yisra-**eil**, ba-aga**la**,
ba-aga**la**, uviz**man** ka**riv**, v'im**ru**: A**mein**.
Ye**hei** shmei ra**ba** m'va**rach** l'a**lam** ul'al**mei** alma**ya**.
Yitba**rach**, v'yishta**bach**, v'yitpa-**ar**, v'yitro**mam**, v'yitna**sei**, v'yit-ha**dar**, v'yit-a**leh**,
v'yit-ha**lal** sh'mei d'kud**sha**, brich hu. L'ei**la** l'ei**la** mi**kol** birchata v'shira**ta**,
tushb'cha**ta** v'nechema**ta** da-ami**ran** b'al**ma**, v'im**ru**: Amein.

God's gloriousness is to be extolled, God's great Name to be hallowed in the world whose creation God willed.
And may God's reign be in our day, during our life, and the life of all Israel, let us say: Amen.
Let God's great Name be praised forever and ever.
Let the Name of the Holy One, the Blessing One, be glorified, exalted, and honored, though God is beyond all the
praises, songs, and adorations that we can utter, and let us say: Amen.

Help us face this coming year Compassionate One.

Help us hold our tempers when they seek to flare.

Help us to be wise and thoughtful and think things through,
Help us to see the good where ever it may surface,
Help us to remember that life is Your precious gift.

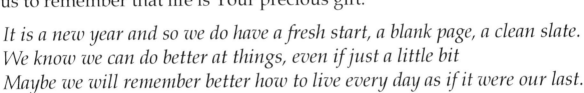

It is a new year and so we do have a fresh start, a blank page, a clean slate.
We know we can do better at things, even if just a little bit
Maybe we will remember better how to live every day as if it were our last.

Let us look at each new day with wonder and gratitude
Let us cherish the memories and the knowledge of sharing
Let us seek You in everyone and every thing.

Help us know what we need to know and not pry where it might hurt.

And most of all, may we be fully present
May we feel Your Presence and acknowledge it every day
May we help others see Your Presence in how we live every day.

As we bless the Source of Life, So we are blessed.
And our blessings give us strength,
and make our visions clear,
and our blessings give us peace,
and the courage to dare,
As we bless the Source of Life, So we are blessed.
© Faith Rogow

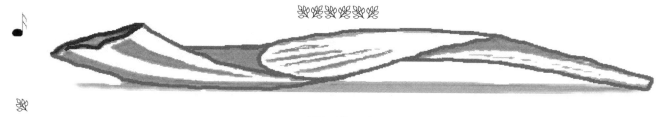

If you are comfortable doing so, please rise and let us sing the 'BAR'CHU'

Bar'chu, Dear One, Shechinah, Holy Name,
When I call on the Light of my Soul, I come home.

Lev Friedman

Bar'chu et Adonai ham'vorach.   בָּרְכוּ אֶת יהוה הַמְבֹרָךְ:

We praise Adonai, the Source of Blessing, Who blesses.

בָּרוּךְ יהוה הַמְבֹרָךְ לְעוֹלָם וָעֶד:

Baruch Adonai hamevorach l'olam va'ed.

Praised be Adonai, the Source of Blessing, now and forever.

Praise the One to whom all praise is due.
Praised be the One to whom all praise is due, Now and forever.
Praise the One to whom all praise is due.
Praised be the One to whom all praise is due
Now and forever, now and forever, now and forever, praise the One. (2x)

We are seated

You are to be praised
Who rolls out the rough, raw clay of the universe
Into delicate vessels of light,
And from nothing at all
Creates the darkness
which lets them shine.
Your vessels pour light upon the universe
Flooding the cracks in our darkness
With the beams of Your compassion.

You are Praised
Who forms from the clay that cloaks our lives,
The delicate vessels
which are our light.

Baruch Ata, Adonai

Eloheinu melech ha-Olam,

yotzeir or, uvorei choshech,

oseh shalom uvorei et hakol.

Baruch Ata Adonai,

yotzeir ham'orot.

בָּרוּךְ אַתָּה יְהֹוָה,
אֱלֹהֵינוּ מֶלֶךְ הָעוֹלָם,
יוֹצֵר אוֹר, וּבוֹרֵא חֹשֶׁךְ,
עֹשֶׂה שָׁלוֹם וּבוֹרֵא אֶת הַכֹּל.
בָּרוּךְ אַתָּה יְהֹוָה,
יוֹצֵר הַמְּאוֹרוֹת:

A Source of Blessing are You, Adonai, our God, Sovereign of the universe, who forms light and creates darkness, makes peace and creates everything.   A Source of Blessing are You, Adonai, our God, Sovereign of the universe, who forms the lights.

We are loved by an unending love,
We are embraced by arms that find us
Even when we are hidden from ourselves.

We are supported by hands that uplift us
even in the midst of a fall.
We are urged on by eyes that meet us
even when we are too weak for meeting.
We are loved by an unending love.

> *Embraced, touched, soothed, and counseled....*
> *ours are the arms, the fingers, the voices;*
> *ours are the hands, the eyes, the smiles;*
> *We are loved by an unending love.*

Blessed are you, Beloved One, who loves your people Israel.   R. Rami M Shapiro

אַהֲבָה רַבָּה אֲהַבְתָּנוּ, יְהֹוָה אֱלֹהֵינוּ, חֶמְלָה גְדוֹלָה וִיתֵרָה חָמַלְתָּ עָלֵינוּ.

Ahava raba ahavtanu Adonai Eloheinu, chemla g'dola viyteira chamalta aleinu.
With abundant love have you loved us, Adonai, our God. With the greatest compassion have you been compassionate to us.

❀❀❀❀❀

Bring us in to peacefulness from the four corners of the earth and grant us independence in our land. And bring us close to You with truth to thank You and proclaim Your Oneness with love.

בָּרוּךְ אַתָּה יהוה, אוֹהֵב עַמּוֹ יִשְׂרָאֵל.

Baruch **a**ta Ado**nai**, o**heiv a**mo Yisra-**eil**.

A Source of Blessing are You, who loves Your people Israel.

❀❀❀❀❀

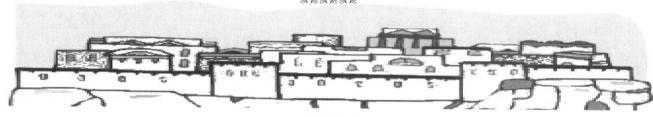

❀❀❀❀❀

I am afraid to dig into the earth of my soul,
for I do not know what I might find there.
I don't know if I have the courage to change, to grow,
to break through the crust of hard soil, of hardened soul.

Whether we plant them or not, the seeds of our future
are sown today for the coming year.
Let us be the planters of our own seeds.
We have no alternative.

To admit that we have failed in the past breaks fresh ground;
To examine our failures is to plant healthy seed,
and to grow from our failures is to stand tall in the garden of growth.

It means saying, "I am sorry."
It means admitting that we have the ability and the need to change,
And this always is embarrassing.

Adonai, help us change our ways -
From callousness to sensitivity, From hostility to love,
From pettiness to purpose, From envy to contentment,
From carelessness to discipline, From fear to faith.

❀❀❀❀❀

Open to me; open your (my) heart; Let my (Your) Presence dwell in you (me).
I am (You are) within you (me), all around you (me), I (You) fill the universe.

❀❀❀❀❀

We are opening up in sweet surrender to the luminous love-light of the One
We are opening.

❀❀❀❀❀

שְׁמַע יִשְׂרָאֵל, יהוה אֱלֹהֵינוּ, יהוה אֶחָד:

Sh'ma Yisra-**eil**: Ado**nai** Elo**hei**nu, Ado**nai Echad!**

Hear, O Israel: Adonai is our God, Adonai is One!

(softly)

בָּרוּךְ שֵׁם כְּבוֹד מַלְכוּתוֹ לְעוֹלָם וָעֶד.

Ba**ruch** sheim ke**vod** male**chu**to le-o**lam** va-**ed!**

Blessed is God's glorious majesty for ever and ever!

✻✻✻✻✻

וְאָהַבְתָּ אֵת יהוה אֱלֹהֶיךָ בְּכָל־לְבָבְךָ וּבְכָל־נַפְשְׁךָ וּבְכָל־מְאֹדֶךָ:
וְהָיוּ הַדְּבָרִים הָאֵלֶּה אֲשֶׁר אָנֹכִי מְצַוְּךָ הַיּוֹם עַל־לְבָבֶךָ: וְשִׁנַּנְתָּם
לְבָנֶיךָ וְדִבַּרְתָּ בָּם בְּשִׁבְתְּךָ בְּבֵיתֶךָ וּבְלֶכְתְּךָ בַדֶּרֶךְ וּבְשָׁכְבְּךָ
וּבְקוּמֶךָ: וּקְשַׁרְתָּם לְאוֹת עַל־יָדֶךָ וְהָיוּ לְטֹטָפֹת בֵּין עֵינֶיךָ:
וּכְתַבְתָּם עַל־מְזֻזוֹת בֵּיתֶךָ וּבִשְׁעָרֶיךָ:

V'ahav**ta** eit Ado**nai** Elo**he**cha; be**chol** levav**cha** uv'**chol** nafshe**cha** uve**chol**
m'o**de**cha. V'ha**yu** had'va**riym** ha'**ei**leh a**sher** Ano**chi** m'tzav**cha** ha**yom** al
leva**ve**cha. V'shinan**tam** l'vane**cha** v'dibar'**ta** bam; b'shiv'te**cha** b'veite**cha**
uv'lechte**cha** vade**rech** uv'shochbe**cha** uvkume**cha**. Ukshar**tam** l'**ot** 'al yade**cha**;
v'ha**yu** l'tota**fot** bein 'ei**ne**cha. Uchtav**tam** 'al-mezu**zot** beite**cha** uvish'are**cha**. (Deut 6:4-9)

✻✻✻✻✻

And thou shalt love the Lord thy God with all of thy heart, with all thy soul, with all
of thy might. And all these words which I command ye on this day will be in thy
heart. And thou shalt teach them diligently unto thy children. And thou shalt
speak of them when thou sittest in thy house, when thou walkest by the way, and
when thou risest up and when thou liest down. And thou shalt bind them for a sign
upon thy hand. And they shall be for frontlets between thine eyes. And thou shalt
bind them on the door posts of thy house, and upon thy gates. That ye may
remember and do all of my commandments and be holy unto thy God.

✻✻✻✻✻

וְאָהַבְתָּ אֵת יהוה אֱלֹהֶיךָ בְּכָל לְבָבְךָ וּבְכָל נַפְשְׁךָ וּבְכָל מְאֹדֶךָ:

V'ahav**ta** eit Ado**nai** Elo**he**cha; be**chol** le**vav**cha uv'**chol** nafshe**cha** uve**chol** m'o**de**cha.

And you will teach your children as you live each day.
The path you walk, the way you talk,
And how you listen for the Good in each soul saying…

וְאָהַבְתָּ אֵת יהוה אֱלֹהֶיךָ

Plant seeds of loving kindness in the fertile soil of faith,
The joy we sow will help us grow
A fragrant Garden of Truth embracing…

וְאָהַבְתָּ אֵת יהוה אֱלֹהֶיךָ

We inscribe these words on the door posts of our being
With heart and mind, we each can find
The precious Light that we are seeking…

וְאָהַבְתָּ אֵת יהוה אֱלֹהֶיךָ

We are all God's children, Living on Mother Earth.
Let hatred cease, bless her with peace.
Become the Mountain, Witness, Holy Wonder birthing…

וְאָהַבְתָּ אֵת יהוה אֱלֹהֶיךָ

© *R. Hanna Tiferet*

🔔 Shema Yisrael

Listen! you Yisrael person
יהוה who is, is our God.

יהוה who is, is One,
unique, all there is.

Through Time and Space
Your Glory Shines Majestic One!

Love, that יהוה who is your God,
in what your heart is in,
in what you aspire to,
in what you have made your own.

May these values
which I connect with your life
be implanted in your feelings.

May they become
the norm for your children,
addressing them
in the privacy of your home,
on the errands you run.

May they help you relax,
and activate you to be productive.

Display them visibly on your arm.
Let them focus your attention.
See them in all transitions,
at home and in your environment.

How good it will be
when you really listen
and hear My directions
which I give you today,
for loving יהוה who is your God,
and acting Godly
with feeling and inspiration.

Your earthly needs will be met
at the right time,
appropriate to the season.
You will reap what you have planted
for your delight and health.

מחזור לחיים

And your animals will have ample feed.
All of you will eat and be content.

Be careful -- watch out!
Don't let your cravings delude you.
Don't become alienated.
Don't let your cravings
become your gods.
Don't debase yourself to them,
because the God-sense within you
will become distorted.
Heaven will be shut to you.
Grace will not descend.
Earth will not produce.
Your rushing will destroy you
and Earth will not be able
to recover her good balance
in which God's gifts manifest.

May these values of Mine
reside in your aspirations
marking what you produce,
guiding what you perceive.

Teach them to your children,
so that they be addressed by them
in making their homes,
how they deal with traffic;
when you are depressed
when you are elated.

Mark your entrances and exits
with them so you are more aware.

Then you and your children
will live out on earth
that divine promise
given to your ancestors

to live heavenly days
right here on this earth.

יהוה who is, said to Moshe
"Speak, telling the Israel folks
to make tzitzit
on the corners of their garments
so they will have
generations to follow them.

On each tzitzit-tassel
let them set a blue thread.
Glance at it,
and in your seeing,
remember all the other directives
of יהוה who is, and act on them.

This way you will not be led astray,
craving to see and want,
and then prostitute yourself
for your cravings.

This way you will be mindful
to actualize My directions
for becoming
dedicated to your God,
to be aware that
I AM
יהוה who is your God --
the One who freed you
from the oppression
in order to God you.

I am יהוה your God."
That is the truth.

Interpretive translation by
Reb Zalman Schachter-Shalomi

יהוה אֱלֹהֵיכֶם: אֱמֶת.. Adonai Eloheichem. Emet..

אֱמֶת וְיַצִּיב וְנָכוֹן וְקַיָּם וְיָשָׁר וְנֶאֱמָן וְאָהוּב וְחָבִיב וְנֶחְמָד וְנָעִים וְנוֹרָא
וְאַדִּיר וּמְתֻקָּן וּמְקֻבָּל וְטוֹב וְיָפֶה הַדָּבָר הַזֶּה עָלֵינוּ לְעוֹלָם וָעֶד.

Emet ve-yatziv vena**chon** vekayam v'yashar v'ne-**eman** v'ahuv v'chaviyv v'nech**mad**
v'na-**iym** v'nora v'adir umtu**kan** umku**bal** v'**tov** v'yafeh hadavar hazeh aleinu le-olam va-ed

True and established, and correct, and upright, and faithful, and beloved, and adored, and desired, and pleasant, and
awesome, and mighty, and powerful, and receiving, and good, and beautiful, is this principal for us forever.

O Mentor of Israel, help us during the coming year
to do all the fine things which we meant to do "some day"
but which we have postponed and neglected.

If we have been waiting to show someone a kindness,
to speak a kind word, to make an overdue call - let us do these things now.
If we have been waiting to perform an act of Tzedakah,
to do a Mitzvah, to assume a responsibility - let us do these things now.

Long ago, Moshe and Miriam had a choice
They could stay in Egypt, the tight place
Where they knew the routine and what was expected of them
Or they could make a change in their lives and the world.

If we have been waiting to cross a sea,
to leave a tight place or uproot a bad habit,
to set aside a festering hatred,
let us do these things now.

May we turn around now and see the miracles around us,
May we join with Moshe and Miriam in their song to God.

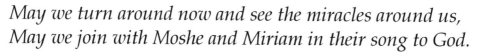

Mi cha**mo**cha ba-ei**lim**, Ado**nai**?   מִי כָמֹכָה בָּאֵלִים יהוה?
Mi ka**mo**cha, ne**dar** bako**desh**,   מִי כָּמֹכָה נֶאְדָּר בַּקֹּדֶשׁ,
no**ra** tehi**lot**, o**sei fe**leh?   נוֹרָא תְהִלֹת, עֹשֵׂה פֶלֶא?
Shi**ra** chada**sha** shib**chu**   שִׁירָה חֲדָשָׁה שִׁבְּחוּ גְאוּלִים לְשִׁמְךָ עַל
ge-u**liym** leshim**cha** al sfat   שְׂפַת הַיָּם, יַחַד כֻּלָּם הוֹדוּ וְהִמְלִיכוּ
ha**yam**, **ya**chad ku**lam ho**du   וְאָמְרוּ: יהוה יִמְלֹךְ לְעוֹלָם וָעֶד:
v'himli**ychu** v'**am**ru: צוּר יִשְׂרָאֵל, קוּמָה בְּעֶזְרַת יִשְׂרָאֵל, וּפְדֵה
"Ado**nai** yim**loch** le-o**lam** va-ed"   כִנְאֻמֶךָ יְהוּדָה וְיִשְׂרָאֵל. גֹּאֲלֵנוּ יהוה
Tzur Yisra-**eil**, **ku**ma b'ez**rat**   צְבָאוֹת שְׁמוֹ, קְדוֹשׁ יִשְׂרָאֵל.
Yisra-**eil** uf**dei** chinu**me**cha   בָּרוּךְ אַתָּה יהוה, גָּאַל יִשְׂרָאֵל עַמֶּךָ:
Yehu**da** v'Yisra-**eil**. Go-a**lei**nu
Ado**nai** Tzeva-**ot** She**mo**,
Ke**dosh** Yisra-**eil**.
Ba**ruch** Ata Ado**nai**, ga-**al**
Yisra-**eil a**me**cha**. (chorus)

Who is like You, Eternal One, among the gods that are worshipped? Who is like You, majestic in holiness, awesome in splendor, doing wonders? The redeemed sang a new song of praise to You on the shores of the sea. Together everyone gave thanks and enthroned You saying: 'Adonai will reign forever and ever.'"
Rock of Israel, rise up and help Israel, redeem us as You promised Judah and Israel. The One whose Name is Adonai Tz'va-ot saves us, the Holy One of Israel. A Source of Blessing are You, Adonai, redeemer of Your people Israel.

Meditation

Our innermost thoughts
are reflected in our body language and action,
even when we think that they are not.
Therefore, speak to yourself only those thoughts
that you want others to see.

Teach me, God, to pray, to bless,
to acknowledge You as the Source of All Life.
Teach me, Adonai, to see the mystery in a flower,
in a tree, in a fruit, sweet and ripe.

> *Teach me, Exalted One, to value life and time,
> morning and night.*

Teach me, Source of Life to treasure life,
lest one day become as any other, not holy.

> *Help me to understand that caring and living fully
> is connecting to Your Essence,
> what the ancients called Hallowing Your Name.*

Help me to fulfill Your expectations as well as my own.
Help me seek You and Your Name, Your Essence.
Please God, help me see the holy.

[The ARK is OPENED]

If you are comfortable doing so, please rise as we open the ark for the Tefilah (the Prayer), the Amidah (the time for standing), the central part of our prayers.

אֲדֹנָי שְׂפָתַי תִּפְתָּח וּפִי יַגִּיד תְּהִלָּתֶךָ:

Adonai sefatai tiftach ufi yagiyd tehilatecha.
Eternal God, open my lips, that my mouth may declare Your glory
Oh, God open up my lips, as I begin to pray.
(Psalm 51:17)

If you are more comfortable sitting, please do so at this time or at any time.

The art on this page is called a shviti and traditionally placed on the Eastern wall of a home or where a person chooses to pray at home. We include it here, at the beginning of the Amidah (central prayer) of our service. If you prefer, you are invited to use it as a meditation device for your private prayers.

🌿🌿🌿🌿🌿

We invoke the memories of our spiritual and physical mothers and fathers who made us, the fathers and the mothers who made them and the fathers and the mothers who made them.

We are the product of all of our ancestors as we
stand here in their light before You who made us all.

Each of them sought You and found You in their lives in different ways.
No two of them experienced You the same way. They are the voices behind us.

🌿🌿🌿🌿🌿

GOD OF ALL GENERATIONS   ♪ אבות

בָּרוּךְ אַתָּה יהוה אֱלֹהֵינוּ וֵאלֹהֵי אֲבוֹתֵינוּ וְאִמּוֹתֵינוּ, אֱלֹהֵי אַבְרָהָם,
אֱלֹהֵי יִצְחָק, וֵאלֹהֵי יַעֲקֹב, אֱלֹהֵי שָׂרָה, אֱלֹהֵי רִבְקָה, אֱלֹהֵי לֵאָה,
וֵאלֹהֵי רָחֵל. הָאֵל הַגָּדוֹל הַגִּבּוֹר וְהַנּוֹרָא, אֵל עֶלְיוֹן, גּוֹמֵל חֲסָדִים
טוֹבִים, וְקוֹנֵה הַכֹּל, וְזוֹכֵר חַסְדֵי אָבוֹת וְאִמָּהוֹת, וּמֵבִיא גְאֻלָּה לִבְנֵי
בְנֵיהֶם לְמַעַן שְׁמוֹ בְּאַהֲבָה:

♪ **Ba**ruch **ata** Adonai, Ehlo**hei**nu, veilo**hei** avo**tei**nu ve-imo**tei**nu: Elo**hei**
Avra**ham**, Elo**hei** Yitz**chak**, vEilo**hei** Ya-a**kov**. Elo**hei** Sarah, Elo**hei** Riv**kah**, Elo**hei**
Lei-**ah**, vEilo**hei** Ra**cheil**. Ha-**eil** haga**dol** hagi**bor** vehano**ra**, eil el**yon**, go**meil**
chasa**dim** to**vim** veko**nei** ha**kol**, V'zo**cheir** chas**dei** a**vot** v'ima**hot**, Umeivi g'u**la**
liv**nei** V'nei**hem**, lema-an sh'**mo**, be-a**hava**:

If you are more comfortable sitting, please do so at this time or at any time.

To Life! High Holy Day Prayer Book

מחזור לחיים

A Source of Blessing are you, Adonai our God and God of our Fathers and our Mothers. God of Abraham, God of Isaac, and God of Jacob, God of Sarah, God of Rebecca, God of Rachel and God of Leah. Great God, powerful and awesome, God of the Highest, who bestows kindness and goodness, master of all, who remembers the good deeds of our fathers and mothers and brings redemption to the children of their children for God's sake with love.

זָכְרֵנוּ לְחַיִּים, מֶלֶךְ חָפֵץ בַּחַיִּים, וְכָתְבֵנוּ בְּסֵפֶר
הַחַיִּים, לְמַעַנְךָ אֱלֹהִים חַיִּים. מֶלֶךְ עוֹזֵר וּמוֹשִׁיעַ וּמָגֵן:
בָּרוּךְ אַתָּה יהוה, מָגֵן אַבְרָהָם וְעֶזְרַת (וּפוֹקֵד) שָׂרָה:

Zoch**rei**nu lecha**yiym**, **Me**lech cha**fetz** bacha**yiym**, vechot**vei**nu be**sei**fer hacha**yiym**, lema-an**cha** Elo**hiym** cha**yiym**. **Me**lech o**zeir** umo**shi**-a uma**gein**: Ba**ruch** A**ta** Ado**nai**, ma**gein** Avra**ham** v'ez**rat** (ufo**keid**) Sa**rah**.

Remember us for life, O Sovereign who favors life, and write us into the Book of Life, for Your sake, O God of Life, Sovereign who is our Help, our redemption and our protector. A Blessing are You, Adonai, Shield of Abraham and Helper of (One who remembers) Sarah.

❧❧❧❧❧❧

Adonai, there was a time for each of us when we felt almost paralyzed with the burdens of life, when everything was overpowering.

We wanted to lie still without moving, feeling almost deadened inside.

And then we turned to You and realized that Your might, Adonai, is everlasting;

Help us use our strength for good and not for evil.

And then we turned to You and realized that You are the support of the falling;

Help us lift up the fallen.

And then we turned to You and realized that You are our hope in death as in life;

Help us keep faith with those who sleep in the dust.

And then we turned to You and realized that Your might, Adonai, is everlasting;

Help us use our strength for good.

Help us to know that it is from you that the radiance comes, that we might rejoice in life itself.

❧❧❧❧❧❧

If you are more comfortable sitting, please do so at this time or at any time.

G'VUROT / POWER
גבורות

אַתָּה גִּבּוֹר לְעוֹלָם אֲדֹנָי מְחַיֵּה הַכֹּל (מֵתִים)
אַתָּה רַב לְהוֹשִׁיעַ:

Atah gibor l'olam Adonai, mechayei hakol (meitiym) Atah, rav lehoshiy'a.

מוֹרִיד הַטָּל:

Moriyd hatal.   Who brings the dew.

מְכַלְכֵּל חַיִּים בְּחֶסֶד, מְחַיֵּה הַכֹּל (מֵתִים)
בְּרַחֲמִים רַבִּים, סוֹמֵךְ נוֹפְלִים, וְרוֹפֵא חוֹלִים, וּמַתִּיר אֲסוּרִים,
וּמְקַיֵּם אֱמוּנָתוֹ לִישֵׁנֵי עָפָר, מִי כָמוֹךָ בַּעַל גְּבוּרוֹת וּמִי דּוֹמֶה לָךְ,
מֶלֶךְ מֵמִית וּמְחַיֶּה וּמַצְמִיחַ יְשׁוּעָה:

Mechalkeil chayim bechesed, mechayei hakol (maytiym) berachamiym rabiym, someich nofliym verofei choliym umatiyr asuriym, um'kayeim emunato liysheinei afar, mi chamocha ba-al gevurot umiy domeh lach, melech meymiyt um'chayeh umatzmiyach yeshu-a.

מִי כָמוֹךָ אַב הָרַחֲמִים, זוֹכֵר יְצוּרָיו לְחַיִּים בְּרַחֲמִים: וְנֶאֱמָן אַתָּה
לְהַחֲיוֹת הַכֹּל (מֵתִים). בָּרוּךְ אַתָּה יהוה, מְחַיֵּה הַכֹּל (מֵתִים):

Mi chamocha Av harachamiym, zocheir yetzurav lechayiym berachamiym.
V'ne-eman Atah lehachayot hakol (maytiym).
Baruch Atah Adonai, mechayei hakol (maytiym).

You are strength forever, Adonai. Giving life to all (the deadened), You are great to save us. You bring the dew. You support life with mercy, You give life to all (the deadened) with great compassion. You support the fallen and heal the sick, You release the captives and establish faith for those who sleep in the dust. Who is like You, master of strength and who can compare to You, Sovereign of life and death, who causes salvation to blossom. Who is like You, compassionate parent, who remembers Your creatures for life with compassion. And You are faithful in giving life to all (the deadened). A Blessing are You, Adonai, who gives life to all (the deadened).

If you are more comfortable sitting, please do so at this time or at any time.

It is easy to look at the U'netanah Tokef as if it is written by someone very old
Or someone stricken with illness,
Pondering imminent death.

And then I watched a plane
Carrying living human beings
Crash into a building
Full of other living human beings.
And the words struck home:

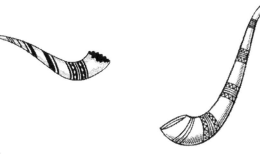

> *Who will live and who will die*
> *Who in due time and who too suddenly*
> *Who by fire and who by water*
> *Who by sword and who by wild beasts (humans)*
> *Who by starvation and who by dehydration*
> *Who by suffocation and who by hurtling objects.*

And I faced the reality of the gift of life and the recognition that it is a gift
Within a moment of time
What was here is gone.

> *Without warning, we can be thrown*
> *Into explosions, implosions*
> *And horrors beyond belief*
> *Amid the screams of those we love.*

And then I watched a child
Walk among those spending time
With a friend or alone;
He blew himself up in that crowd
And killed those around him
And the words struck home:

> *Who will live and who will die*
> *Who in due time and who too suddenly*
> *Who by fire and who by water*
> *Who by sword and who by wild beasts (humans)*
> *Who by starvation and who by dehydration*
> *Who by suffocation and who by hurtling objects.*

And I faced the reality of the gift of life and the recognition that it is a gift
Within a moment of time
What was here is gone.
If you are more comfortable sitting, please do so at this time or at any time.

Rosh HaShanah

And I watched as Fire
Devoured trees and homes
Destroying all in its path.

And I watched as storms
Pelted the shores,
Drowning those who lingered
In its path too long.

And I watched as cars
Collided with each other
And rolled and crashed.

And I watched as children and adults,
Too thin to eat
Wasted away in lands
Too near and too far away to name.

And the words struck home:

> Who will live and who will die
> Who in due time and who too suddenly

> *And I heard people asking why God allowed such things*
> *And I heard people ask where God was, were we abandoned.*

And I realized that God gave us the answers within our Self
If we would only look and do the work.

Perhaps the bitterness of the decree
May be sweetened
By turning into oneself and examining deeds and thoughts

> *By turning to God for Divine inspiration*
> *By turning to others and doing God's work*
> *With our own hands and our own words*

May we find a way this year
To cleanse ourselves of bitterness and anger
To lift up our hearts and minds to Godliness

> *May we seek righteousness*
> *May we seek love*
> *May we seek the Divine in all of us.*

May we hear the Shofar,   May we LIVE LIFE this year.

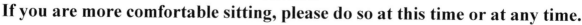

If you are more comfortable sitting, please do so at this time or at any time.

UNTANEH TOKEF   וּנְתַנֶּה תֹּקֶף

וּנְתַנֶּה תֹּקֶף קְדֻשַּׁת הַיּוֹם, כִּי הוּא נוֹרָא וְאָיוֹם: וּבוֹ תִנָּשֵׂא מַלְכוּתֶךָ,
וְיִכּוֹן בְּחֶסֶד כִּסְאֶךָ, וְתֵשֵׁב עָלָיו בֶּאֱמֶת. אֱמֶת כִּי אַתָּה הוּא דַיָּן
וּמוֹכִיחַ, וְיוֹדֵעַ וָעֵד, וְכוֹתֵב וְחוֹתֵם, וְסוֹפֵר וּמוֹנֶה, וְתִזְכּוֹר כָּל הַנִּשְׁכָּחוֹת:
וְתִפְתַּח אֶת סֵפֶר הַזִּכְרוֹנוֹת, וּמֵאֵלָיו יִקָּרֵא, וְחוֹתָם יַד כָּל אָדָם בּוֹ.

Untaneh tokef kedushat hayom, ki hu nora ve-ayom: uvo tinasei malchutecha, v'yikon bechesed kis'echa, veteisheiv alav be-emet. Emet ki Ata Hu dayan umochiyach, veyodei-a va-eid, vechoteiv vechoteim, vesofeir umoneh, vetizkor kol hanishkachot: vetiftach et seifer hazichronot, umei-eilav yikarei, vechotam yad kol adam bo.

We acclaim this day's pure sanctity, its awesome power. You record and seal, count and measure, remembering all that we have forgotten. You open the Book of Remembrance and it speaks for itself, for every person has signed it personally.

The great shofar is sounded. A still, small voice is heard. This day even angels are alert, filled with awe and trembling as they declare: "The day of judgment is here!" For even the hosts of heaven are judged. This day all who walk the earth pass before You as a flock of sheep. And like a shepherd who gathers the flock, bringing them under the staff, You bring everything that lives before You for review. You determine life and decree the destiny of every creature.

בְּרֹאשׁ הַשָּׁנָה יִכָּתֵבוּן, וּבְיוֹם צוֹם כִּפּוּר יֵחָתֵמוּן.

BeRosh HaShanah yikateivun. Uv'Yom Tzom Kippur yeichateimun.
On Rosh Hashanah it is written And on Yom Kippur it is sealed:

How many will leave this world and how many will be born into it, who will live and who will die, who will live in fullness and who will not, who by fire and who by water, who by sword and who by beast, who by hunger and who by thirst, who by earthquake and who by plague, who by strangling and who by stoning, who will rest and who will wander, who will be at peace and who will be tormented, who will be poor and who will be rich, who will be humbled and who will be exalted.

וּתְשׁוּבָה וּתְפִלָּה וּצְדָקָה מַעֲבִירִין אֶת רֹעַ הַגְּזֵרָה.

Ut'shuvah ut'filah utzedakah ma-aviriyn et ro-a hagzeirah.
And returning to God, prayer and tzedakah avert the harshness of the decree.

If you are more comfortable sitting, please do so at this time or at any time.

To Life! High Holy Day Prayer Book   מחזור לחיים

Nekadesh/Kedushah/Holiness   נקדש\קדושה

נְקַדֵּשׁ אֶת שִׁמְךָ בָּעוֹלָם, כְּשֵׁם שֶׁמַּקְדִּישִׁים אוֹתוֹ בִּשְׁמֵי מָרוֹם,

כַּכָּתוּב עַל יַד נְבִיאֶךָ, וְקָרָא זֶה אֶל זֶה וְאָמַר:

Nekadeish et shimcha ba-olam k'sheim shemakdiyshiym oto bish'mei marom,
kakatuv al yad n'vi-echa v'kara zeh el zeh v'amar:

We sanctify Your name for all time and space, just as Your Holy Name was sanctified in the highest places, as it was written by the hand of Your prophets, and they [the angels] called out to each other:

קָדוֹשׁ קָדוֹשׁ קָדוֹשׁ יהוה צְבָאוֹת, מְלֹא כָל הָאָרֶץ כְּבוֹדוֹ.

Kadosh kadosh kadosh Adonai Tz'va-ot, melo chol ha-aretz kevodo.
Holy, Holy, Holy are You, Adonai Tz'va-ot, all the earth is filled with Your glory.

אַדִּיר אַדִּירֵנוּ, יהוה אֲדֹנֵינוּ, מָה אַדִּיר שִׁמְךָ בְּכָל הָאָרֶץ.

Adiyr adiyreinu, Adonai Adoneinu, mah adiyr shimcha bechol ha-aretz.
Strength of our strength, connectivity of our connectivity, how mighty is Your Name in all the earth.

בָּרוּךְ כְּבוֹד יהוה, מִמְּקוֹמוֹ.

Baruch kevod Adonai mimkomo.
A source of Blessing is Adonai's glory, radiating from the Source.

אֶחָד הוּא אֱלֹהֵינוּ, הוּא אָבִינוּ, הוּא מַלְכֵּנוּ, הוּא מוֹשִׁיעֵנוּ, וְהוּא

יַשְׁמִיעֵנוּ בְּרַחֲמָיו שֵׁנִית לְעֵינֵי כָּל חַי:

Hu Eloheinu, Hu Avinu, Hu Malkeinu, Hu Moshi-einu, veHu Yashmi-einu berachamav sheiniyt l'einei kol chai.

One is our God, God is our parent, God is our Sovereign, God is our salvation. And God will declare again with compassion for the eyes of all that live:

אֲנִי יהוה אֱלֹהֵיכֶם!

Ani Adonai Eloheichem
I am Adonai your God.

יִמְלֹךְ יהוה לְעוֹלָם, אֱלֹהַיִךְ צִיּוֹן לְדֹר וָדֹר, הַלְלוּיָהּ.

Yimloch Adonai l'olam, elohayich tziyon ledor vador. Hallelu-Yahh.
Adonai will reign forever, Your God, Tzion, from generation to generation. Praise Yahh (Adonai).

לְדוֹר וָדוֹר נַגִּיד גָּדְלֶךָ וּלְנֵצַח נְצָחִים קְדֻשָּׁתְךָ נַקְדִּישׁ, וְשִׁבְחֲךָ

אֱלֹהֵינוּ מִפִּינוּ לֹא יָמוּשׁ לְעוֹלָם וָעֶד, כִּי אֵל מֶלֶךְ גָּדוֹל וְקָדוֹשׁ אָתָּה.

L'dor vador nagiyd godlecha ul'neitzach n'tzachiym kedushatcha nakdiysh.
V'shivchacha Eloheinu mipinu lo yamush l'olam va-ed. Ki Eil Melech gadol
vekadosh Atah.

We sing and praise the Holy One.

For the children and their children, (We) bless the Light.

If you are more comfortable sitting, please do so at this time or at any time.

From generation to generation, we will tell of Your greatness and for all time we will sanctify Your holiness. O God, Your praise will never vanish from our lips, for you are a great and Holy Divine Sovereign.

אַתָּה קָדוֹשׁ וְשִׁמְךָ קָדוֹשׁ וּקְדוֹשִׁים בְּכָל יוֹם יְהַלְלוּךָ, סֶּלָה.

Ata kadosh veshim**cha** ka**dosh** ukdo**shiym** be**chol** yom yehale**lu**cha, **Se**la.

You are holiness and Your Name is Holy, we praise your holiness every day, Selah.

U'VECHEIN

וכן

U'vechein, Make all creatures awestruck at Your greatness. Help all life align their desires with Yours, with full harmony of heart, sharing in Your glory. Bring us hope in Your promise, joy in our land, delight in Your city, Jerusalem.

Then Your power will be the only one we know, and holiness will rule from the City of Peace, Your Shechina's dwelling. So we sing:

יִמְלֹךְ יהוה לְעוֹלָם, אֱלֹהַיִךְ צִיּוֹן לְדֹר וָדֹר: הַלְלוּיָהּ.

All: *Yimloch Adonai l'olam, Elohayich Tzion, Ledor vador, HalleluYahh!*
Holy Awesome One! There is none like You!
You have chosen us to serve You by loving us and giving us Your guidance through Torah and mitzvot, through which we link ourselves to You.

R. Marcia Prager, adapted

בָּרוּךְ אַתָּה יהוה, הַמֶּלֶךְ הַקָּדוֹשׁ.

Baruch A**ta**, Ado**nai** ha-**Me**lech ha**Ka**dosh.
A Blessing are You, Adonai, the Holy Sovereign.

We are seated.

When we look at a flower, we can see You, God.
When we look at a sleeping child, You are there, too.
Your Presence is in the hugs and smiles from friends and loved ones.

Life abounds and we are the ones who distance ourselves.
We are the ones who hide from You.
We hide from You by hiding from ourselves
By hiding from the things we know we need to do.

Help us, God, to do what needs to be done,
To feel what needs to be felt,
To know what needs to be known,
So that we can be what we need to be.

מחזור לחיים

If Rosh HaShanah falls on Shabbat, please add { }:

בָּרוּךְ אַתָּה יהוה, מְקַדֵּשׁ {הַשַׁבָּת וְ} יִשְׂרָאֵל וְיוֹם הַזִּכָּרוֹן:

Baruch **A**ta Ado**nai**, meka**deish** {ha**Sha**bat v'}Yisra-**eil** ve**yom** hazika**ron**.

A Blessing are You, Adonai, who makes holy {the Shabbat and} Israel and this day of Remembering.

❧❧❧❧❧

On this Day of Remembering, God,
Remember us for our good and for blessing,
Save us for fullness of life,
Grant us victory over our smallness, And peace.
> *Adonai, our God, Let this holy time*
> *Lift us to Your presence in life, in peace, in joy.*

May we find rest in our rest,
Holiness in our performance of mitzvot.
May we, Your people Israel, find You.

❧❧❧❧❧

בָּרוּךְ אַתָּה יהוה, הַמַּחֲזִיר שְׁכִינָתוֹ לְצִיּוֹן.

Baruch **A**ta Ado**nai**, hamacha**zir** shechi**na**to l'tzi**yon**.

A Source of Blessing are You, Adonai, who returns Shechina to Tzion.

❧❧❧❧❧

Thank You for the gift of life.
Thank You for the new year
and the fresh start that gives us.
Each one of us leads imperfect lives,
The children of our own parents' imperfections

And those of humanity.
Thank You for forgiving us when we do fail,
and for the chance to start fresh this year.
Thank You for the gift of Your Love and of Hope,
Thank You for Your Loving and Forgiving Presence
in our lives.

> ❧❧❧❧❧ ❧❧❧❧❧
> Meditation
> God did not create
> a completed world.
> Rather, God gave us
> a purpose in life
> and challenges
> to make ourselves
> and the world whole.
> Rabbi Sholom Silver
> (1921-1974)
> ❧❧❧❧❧ ❧❧❧❧❧

> *Inscribe all Israel and all humankind*
> *For a good life, For a life of living.*
> *Thank You for it all.*

❧❧❧❧❧ ❧❧❧❧❧

בָּרוּךְ אַתָּה יהוה, הַטּוֹב שִׁמְךָ וּלְךָ נָאֶה לְהוֹדוֹת.

Baruch **A**ta Ado**nai**, ha**tov** shim**cha** ule**cha** na-**eh** leho**dot**.

A Source of Blessing are You, Adonai, whose Essence is goodness and who is worthy of our thanks.

❧❧❧❧❧

יְבָרֶכְךָ יהוה וְיִשְׁמְרֶךָ.   כֵּן יְהִי רָצוֹן

Y'varech'cha Adonai v'yishmerecha.   Kein yehi ratzon.

May Adonai bless you and protect you.

יָאֵר יהוה פָּנָיו אֵלֶיךָ וִיחֻנֶּךָּ.   כֵּן יְהִי רָצוֹן

Ya-eir Adonai panav eilecha vichuneka.   Kein yehi ratzon.

May Adonai shine God's countenance on you with wisdom and grace.

יִשָּׂא יהוה פָּנָיו אֵלֶיךָ וְיָשֵׂם לְךָ שָׁלוֹם.   כֵּן יְהִי רָצוֹן

Yisa Adonai panav eilecha v'yaseim lecha shalom.   Kein yehi ratzon.

May Adonai lift God's countenance onto you and grant you shalom, peace and wholeness.

We offer to You again, the prayer for peace:

"Peace to those near and to those far off."

For the Prophets teach: If others are in turmoil and

disharmony rules their lives, there can be no peace for us.

When the noise of our lives drowns out the music for which we yearn,

others likewise can find no peace.

שָׁלוֹם

Peace for all Israel. Peace for all humankind.

בָּרוּךְ אַתָּה יהוה, עוֹשֶׂה הַשָּׁלוֹם.

Baruch Ata Adonai, oseh hashalom.

Blessings are You, Adonai, who makes peace.

WE PRAY SILENTLY

עֹשֶׂה שָׁלוֹם בִּמְרוֹמָיו הוּא יַעֲשֶׂה שָׁלוֹם עָלֵינוּ וְעַל כָּל יִשְׂרָאֵל,
(וְעַל כָּל יוֹשְׁבֵי תֵבֵל.) וְאִמְרוּ אָמֵן:

Oseh shalom bimromav, hu ya-aseh shalom aleinu, v'al kol Yisra-eil, (v'al kol
yoshvei teyveil,) v'imru: amein.

May the One who makes peace in the high places, make peace for us and for Israel and
all the world, and let us say, Amen.

שְׁמַע קוֹלֵנוּ, יהוה אֱלֹהֵינוּ, חוּס וְרַחֵם עָלֵינוּ, וְקַבֵּל בְּרַחֲמִים
וּבְרָצוֹן אֶת תְּפִלָּתֵנוּ. כִּי אֵל שׁוֹמֵעַ תְּפִלּוֹת וְתַחֲנוּנִים אָתָּה.

Sh'ma koleinu, Adonai Eloheinu, chus v'racheim aleinu, v'kabeil berachamiym
uvratzon et tefilateinu. Ki Eil shomei-a tefilot v'tachanuniym Ata.

Hear our voice, Adonai our God. Have pity and mercy on us and receive our prayers with compassion
and favor. For You are a God who listens to prayers and supplications.

[The ARK is OPENED]

If you are comfortable doing so, please rise as we open the ark for Avinu Malkeinu

אָבִינוּ מַלְכֵּנוּ! שְׁמַע קוֹלֵנוּ.

Avinu Malkeinu! Sh'ma koleinu.

Avinu Malkeynu! Hear our plea.

אָבִינוּ מַלְכֵּנוּ! חָטָאנוּ לְפָנֶיךָ.

Avinu Malkeinu! Chatanu lefanecha.

Avinu Malkeynu! We have sinned.

אָבִינוּ מַלְכֵּנוּ! חֲמוֹל עָלֵינוּ וְעַל עוֹלָלֵנוּ וְטַפֵּנוּ.

Avinu Malkeinu! Chamol aleinu v'al olaleinu vetapeinu.

Avinu Malkeynu! Have mercy on us and on our children.

אָבִינוּ מַלְכֵּנוּ! כַּלֵּה דֶבֶר וְחֶרֶב וְרָעָב מֵעָלֵינוּ.

Avinu Malkeinu! Kalei dever v'cherev v'ra'av mey-aleinu.

Avinu Malkeynu! Help us diminish pestilence, war and famine.

אָבִינוּ מַלְכֵּנוּ! כַּלֵּה כָּל צַר וּמַשְׂטִין מֵעָלֵינוּ.

Avinu Malkeinu! Kalei kol tzar umistiyn mei-aleinu.

Avinu Malkeynu! Help us diminish hate and oppresion.

אָבִינוּ מַלְכֵּנוּ! כָּתְבֵנוּ בְּסֵפֶר חַיִּים טוֹבִים.

Avinu Malkeinu! Kotveinu beseifer chayiym toviym.

Avinu Malkeynu! Enter us into the Book of Life

אָבִינוּ מַלְכֵּנוּ! חַדֵּשׁ עָלֵינוּ שָׁנָה טוֹבָה.

Avinu Malkeinu! Chadeish aleinu shanah tovah.

Avinu Malkeynu! Renew our faith in the future that we may make the coming year truly a shanah tovah, a year of goodness.

אָבִינוּ מַלְכֵּנוּ! חָנֵּנוּ וַעֲנֵנוּ, כִּי אֵין בָּנוּ מַעֲשִׂים, עֲשֵׂה עִמָּנוּ צְדָקָה וָחֶסֶד וְהוֹשִׁיעֵנוּ.

Avinu Malkeinu! Chaneinu va'aneinu, ki ein banu ma-asiym, asei imanu tzedakah vachesed vehoshi-einu.

Avinu Malkeynu! Please be gracious and answer us, for we have not earned it; please help us to do right through Tzedakah and be a conduit for Your mercy that we might become worthy.

We are seated.

TORAH SERVICE

If you are comfortable doing so, please rise as we open the ark for the Torah

כִּי מִצִּיּוֹן תֵּצֵא תוֹרָה , וּדְבַר יהוה מִירוּשָׁלָיִם:

בָּרוּךְ שֶׁנָּתַן תּוֹרָה לְעַמּוֹ יִשְׂרָאֵל בִּקְדֻשָּׁתוֹ:

Ki mi-tzi**yon** tei**tzei** to**rah**, ud'var Ado**nai** mirusha**la**yim.
Baruch she-na**tan** to**rah** l'**amo** Yisra-**eil** bik'dusha**to**.

For from Tzion, Torah goes forth and the word of Adonai from Jerusalem.
A Source of Blessing is the One who gave Torah to God's people Israel in holiness.

יהוה, יהוה, אֵל רַחוּם וְחַנּוּן, אֶרֶךְ אַפַּיִם, וְרַב חֶסֶד

וֶאֱמֶת: נֹצֵר חֶסֶד לָאֲלָפִים, נֹשֵׂא עָוֹן וָפֶשַׁע וְחַטָּאָה, וְנַקֵּה:

Ado**nai** Ado**nai** eil ra**chum** vecha**nun**, erech a**pa**yim ve**rav** che**sed** ve-e**met**,
no**tzeir** che**sed** la-ala**fiym**, no**sei** a**von** va**fe**sha vechata-**ah** vena**kei**.

Adonai, Adonai, God of compassion and grace, slow to anger and abounding with mercy and truth.
You grant mercy to the thousands, lifting shame and inequity and sin; You are cleansing.

(The Torah is removed from the Ark.)

CALL AND RESPONSE (leader, then congregation):

שְׁמַע יִשְׂרָאֵל, יהוה אֱלֹהֵינוּ, יהוה אֶחָד.

She**ma** Yisra-**eil,** Ado**nai** Elo**hei**nu, Ado**nai** e**chad**!

Hear, O Israel, Adonai is our God, Adonai is One.

אֶחָד אֱלֹהֵינוּ, גָּדוֹל אֲדוֹנֵנוּ, קָדוֹשׁ וְנוֹרָא שְׁמוֹ.

E**chad** Elo**hei**nu ga**dol** ado**nei**nu ka**dosh** veno**rah** Sh'**mo**.

Our God is One; Adonai is great; holy and awesome is God's Name.

Together:

גַּדְּלוּ לַיהוה אִתִּי, וּנְרוֹמְמָה שְׁמוֹ יַחְדָּו.

Gad**lu** l'Ado**nai** iti, un'rom'**mah** sh'**mo** yach'**dav**.

Acknowledge Adonai's greatness with me, and let us exalt God's Name together.

לְךָ יהוה הַגְּדֻלָּה וְהַגְּבוּרָה וְהַתִּפְאֶרֶת וְהַנֵּצַח וְהַהוֹד, כִּי כֹל

בַּשָּׁמַיִם וּבָאָרֶץ: לְךָ יהוה הַמַּמְלָכָה וְהַמִּתְנַשֵּׂא לְכֹל לְרֹאשׁ.

Lecha Ado**nai** hagedu**la** vehagevu**ra** vehatif-**e**ret vehanei**tzach** veha**hod**, ki
chol basha**ma**yim uva-**a**retz: **Le**cha Ado**nai** hamamla**cha** vehamitna**sei** le**chol**
le**rosh**.

Yours, Adonai, is the greatness, the power, the glory, the victory, and the majesty; for all that is in
heaven and earth is Yours. Yours is the kingdom, Adonai, You are supreme over all.

עַל שְׁלשָׁה דְבָרִים הָעוֹלָם עוֹמֵד, עַל הַתּוֹרָה וְעַל
הָעֲבוֹדָה וְעַל גְּמִילוּת חֲסָדִים

Al shlo**sha** deva**riym**, ha-**o**lam **o**meid.
Al ha**To**rah v'**al** ha-avo**dah**, v'**al** gemi**lut** chasa**diym**.
The world depends on three things: on Torah, on worship and on loving deeds.

Once the Torah is resting on the table, we are seated.

TORAH BLESSING (Before Reading)

בָּרְכוּ אֶת יהוה הַמְבוֹרָךְ.

Barchu et Ado**nai** hamevo**rach**.
We praise Adonai, the Source of Blessing, Who blesses.

בָּרוּךְ יהוה הַמְבוֹרָךְ לְעוֹלָם וָעֶד:

Ba**ruch** Ado**nai** hamevo**rach** l'**o**lam va-**ed**.
Praised be Adonai, the Source of Blessing, now and forever.

בָּרוּךְ אַתָּה יהוה אֱלֹהֵינוּ מֶלֶךְ הָעוֹלָם, אֲשֶׁר בָּחַר בָּנוּ עִם
(מִ-)כָּל הָעַמִּים וְנָתַן לָנוּ אֶת תּוֹרָתוֹ:
בָּרוּךְ אַתָּה יהוה, נוֹתֵן הַתּוֹרָה.

Ba**ruch** A**ta** Ado**nai**, Elo**hei**nu **Me**lech ha-**o**lam **a**sher ba**char ba**nu im
(mi)**kol** ha-a**miym**, Vena**tan la**nu et Tora**to**. Ba**ruch** A**ta** Ado**nai**, no**tein** ha**To**rah.
Blessed is Adonai, our God, Sovereign of the universe, who has chosen us with (from) all peoples and has given us Torah. A Source of Blessing is Adonai, Giver of the Torah.

Torah Reading

א וַיְהִי אַחַר הַדְּבָרִים הָאֵלֶּה וְהָאֱלֹהִים נִסָּה
אֶת־אַבְרָהָם וַיֹּאמֶר אֵלָיו אַבְרָהָם וַיֹּאמֶר הִנֵּנִי:

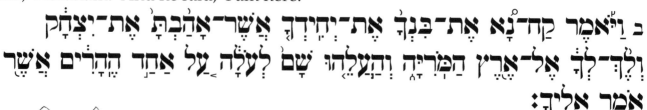

Vaye**hi** a**char** hadeva**riym** ha'**ei**leh veha'Elo**hiym** ni**sa** et
Avra**ham** vayo**mer** ei**lav** "Avra**ham**" vayo**mer** "hi**nei**ni."
22:1 After these events, Elohiym tested Abraham and said to
him, 'Abraham!' And he said, 'I am here.'

ב וַיֹּאמֶר קַח־נָא אֶת־בִּנְךָ אֶת־יְחִידְךָ אֲשֶׁר־אָהַבְתָּ אֶת־יִצְחָק
וְלֶךְ־לְךָ אֶל־אֶרֶץ הַמֹּרִיָּה וְהַעֲלֵהוּ שָׁם לְעֹלָה עַל אַחַד הֶהָרִים אֲשֶׁר
אֹמַר אֵלֶיךָ:

Vayo**mer** kach na et bin**cha** et yechiy**dcha** **a**sher ahav**ta** et
Yitz**chak** ve**lech** le**cha** el **e**retz ha**Mo**riah veha'**a**lehu sham
le'**o**lah al a**chad** heha**riym** **a**sher o**mar** e**lecha**.

22:2 And God said, "Take your son, your only one, the one you have loved, Isaac. And go for yourself to the Moriah area. Bring an offering there on one of the mountains that I will designate to you."

ג וַיַּשְׁכֵּם אַבְרָהָם בַּבֹּקֶר וַיַּחֲבֹשׁ אֶת־חֲמֹרוֹ וַיִּקַּח אֶת־שְׁנֵי נְעָרָיו אִתּוֹ וְאֵת יִצְחָק בְּנוֹ וַיְבַקַּע עֲצֵי עֹלָה וַיָּקָם וַיֵּלֶךְ אֶל־הַמָּקוֹם אֲשֶׁר־אָמַר־לוֹ הָאֱלֹהִים:

Vayash**keim** Avra**ham** ba**bo**ker vayacha**vosh** et-chamo**ro** vayi**kach** et shnei ne'**arav** ito ve'**et** Yitz**chak** be**no** vaiva**ka** atzei o**lah** vaya**kom** vaye**lech** el hama**kom** asher **a**mar lo ha'Elo**hiym**.

22:3 So Abraham got up early in the morning and saddled his donkey. And he took his two youths with him, and Isaac, his son. He cut wood for the offering, and set out and went to the place about which Elohiym told him.

❋❋❋❋❋

ט וַיָּבֹאוּ אֶל־הַמָּקוֹם אֲשֶׁר אָמַר־לוֹ הָאֱלֹהִים וַיִּבֶן שָׁם אַבְרָהָם אֶת־הַמִּזְבֵּחַ וַיַּעֲרֹךְ אֶת־הָעֵצִים וַיַּעֲקֹד אֶת־יִצְחָק בְּנוֹ וַיָּשֶׂם אֹתוֹ עַל־הַמִּזְבֵּחַ מִמַּעַל לָעֵצִים:

Vaya**vo**'u el hama**kom** asher **a**mar lo ha'Elo**hiym** vayi**ven** sham Avra**ham** et hamiz**bei**'ach vaya'**aroch** et ha'**etziym** vaya'**akod** et Yitz**chak** be**no** vaya**sem** o**to** al hamiz**bei**'ach mi**ma**'al la'ei**tziym**.

22:9 And they came to the place that Elohiym had told him about. Abraham built the altar there, and arranged the wood. He then bound Isaac, his son, and placed him on the altar on top of the wood.

י וַיִּשְׁלַח אַבְרָהָם אֶת־יָדוֹ וַיִּקַּח אֶת־הַמַּאֲכֶלֶת לִשְׁחֹט אֶת־בְּנוֹ:

Vayish**lach** Avra**ham** et ya**do** vayi**kach** et hama'**achel**et lish**chot** et be**no**.

22:10 Abraham reached out and took the slaughter knife into his hand to slaughter his son.

יא וַיִּקְרָא אֵלָיו מַלְאַךְ יהוה מִן־הַשָּׁמַיִם וַיֹּאמֶר אַבְרָהָם | אַבְרָהָם וַיֹּאמֶר הִנֵּנִי:

Vayik**ra** eilav mal'**ach** Adonai min hasha**ma**yim vayo**mer**, "Avra**ham** Avra**ham**" vayo**mer** "hi**nei**ni."

22:11 Adonai's angel called to him from the heavens and said, 'Abraham! Abraham!' And he said, 'I am here.'

יב וַיֹּאמֶר אַל־תִּשְׁלַח יָדְךָ אֶל־הַנַּעַר וְאַל־תַּעַשׂ לוֹ
מְאוּמָה כִּי | עַתָּה יָדַעְתִּי כִּי־יְרֵא אֱלֹהִים אַתָּה וְלֹא
חָשַׂכְתָּ אֶת־בִּנְךָ אֶת־יְחִידְךָ מִמֶּנִּי:

Vayomer al tishlach yadcha el hana'ar ve'al ta'as lo
me'umah ki atah yada'ti ki yerei Elohiym atah velo
chasachta et bincha et yechidcha mimeni.

22:12 And he said, 'Do not put forth your hand toward the boy. Do not make a
waste of him. For now I know that you perceive God. You have not withheld
your only son from Me.'

❧❧❧❧❧

TORAH BLESSING (After Reading)

בָּרוּךְ אַתָּה יהוה אֱלֹהֵינוּ מֶלֶךְ הָעוֹלָם, אֲשֶׁר נָתַן לָנוּ תּוֹרַת
אֱמֶת, וְחַיֵּי עוֹלָם נָטַע בְּתוֹכֵנוּ. בָּרוּךְ אַתָּה יהוה, נוֹתֵן הַתּוֹרָה.

**Baruch Ata Adonai Eloheinu Melech ha-olam, asher natan lanu torat emet,
vechayei olam nata betocheinu. Baruch Ata Adonai notein haTorah.**
A Source of Blessing is Adonai, our God, Sovereign of the universe, who has given us a Torah of truth,
implanting it within us. A Source of Blessing is Adonai, Giver of the Torah.

❧❧❧❧❧

Prayer for healing

מִי שֶׁבֵּרַךְ אֲבוֹתֵינוּ מְקוֹר הַבְּרָכָה לְאִמּוֹתֵינוּ

Mi shebeirach avoteinu mekor habracha le-imoteinu.
May the source of strength who blessed the ones before us
Help us find the courage to make our lives a blessing. And let us say -- Amen.

מִי שֶׁבֵּרַךְ אִמּוֹתֵינוּ מְקוֹר הַבְּרָכָה לַאֲבוֹתֵינוּ

Mi shebeirach imoteinu mekor habracha la-avoteinu.
Bless those in need of healing with r'fua sh'leima
the renewal of body, the renewal of spirit.   And let us say -- Amen.
© Debbie Friedman

❧❧❧❧❧

    El na refa na lahh   אֵל נָא רְפָא נָא לָה

❧❧❧❧❧

בָּרוּךְ אַתָּה יהוה, שֶׁגְּמָלַנִי כָּל טוֹב:

Baruch Ata Yah (Adonai), shegmalani kol tov.
Humbly I stand before You today, blessed with the gift of life.

מִי שֶׁגְּמָלֵךְ (שֶׁגְּמָלְךָ) כָּל טוֹב, יִגְמָלֵךְ (יִגְמָלְךָ) כָּל טוֹב סֶלָה:

Mi shegmaleich (shegmalcha) kol tov, yigmaleich (yigmalcha) kol tov selah.
note: female (male)

❧❧❧❧❧

If you are comfortable doing so, please rise as we lift and dress the Torah

וְזֹאת הַתּוֹרָה אֲשֶׁר שָׂם מֹשֶׁה
לִפְנֵי בְּנֵי יִשְׂרָאֵל עַל פִּי יהוה בְּיַד מֹשֶׁה:

Vezot haTorah asher sam Moshe lifnei benei Yisra-eil al pi Adonai beyad Moshe.

This is the Torah that Moses placed before the people of Israel, the word of Adonai.

❀❀❀❀

We are seated

❀❀❀❀

SHOFAR SERVICE

תִּקְעוּ בַחֹדֶשׁ שׁוֹפָר, בַּכֶּסֶה לְיוֹם חַגֵּנוּ.
כִּי חֹק לְיִשְׂרָאֵל הוּא, מִשְׁפָּט לֵאלֹהֵי יַעֲקֹב.

Tik'u vachodesh shofar, bakeseh leyom chageynu.
Ki chok, l'Yisra-eil hu, mishpat ley'lohei Ya-akov.

Blast on the Shofar for the new month, at the setting for our Festival.
For it is a statute for Israel and a decree for the God of Ya-akov.

❀❀❀❀

The Shofar we hear today
is the Shofar from the ram
caught in the thicket behind Abraham,
which he offered in place of his son.
Through the ages it connects us with both of them;
the parent striving and failing, the child wondering why.
Will we see the angel in time when it is our turn?
Will we know what to ask?
Will we learn how to do the things that matter
when they matter most?

❀❀❀❀

מִן הַמֵּצַר קָרָאתִי יָהּ, עֲנָנִי בַמֶּרְחַב יָהּ.

Min ha**mei**tzar kara'ti Yahh, **an**ani bamer**chav** Yahh.
Out of my distress I called out "Adonai (Yah)" God (Yah) answered me and set me free.

For generations, on this day, our ancestors listened to the sound of the Shofar.

Tekiah! Awake! DO NOT let habit dull your minds,
Examine your deeds, look well into your soul, mend your ways, turn to God.

Shevariym! The broken refrain! Listen to the staccato cry.

Hear the echoes of sighing and weeping.
The deprived and the distressed, the neglected and the
enslaved, the bruised and the broken.
All cry out for relief from their pain, for release from their torment.

Teruah! The call to battle is sounded: Join the struggle against evil and suffering.
Give of your bread to those who hunger;
give of your strength to those who stumble;
heal the wounded; comfort the bereaved.

בָּרוּךְ אַתָּה, יהוה אֱלֹהֵינוּ, מֶלֶךְ הָעוֹלָם, אֲשֶׁר קִדְּשָׁנוּ בְּמִצְוֹתָיו,
וְצִוָּנוּ לִשְׁמֹעַ קוֹל שׁוֹפָר.

Ba**ruch** ata Ado**nai** Elo**hey**nu **Me**lech ha-o**lam**, **asher** kid**sha**nu b'mitzvo**tav**,
Vetzi**va**nu, lish**mo**-a kol sho**far**.
The Source of Blessing are You, Eternal Sovereign.
You make us special with Mitzvot and instruct us to hear the voice of the Shofar.

Today we stand before You to affirm our faith in the Holy One, to God for giving
us life, for sustaining us, and for enabling us to reach this season. Amen!

בָּרוּךְ אַתָּה יהוה אֱלֹהֵינוּ מֶלֶךְ הָעוֹלָם,
שֶׁהֶחֱיָנוּ וְקִיְּמָנוּ וְהִגִּיעָנוּ לַזְּמַן הַזֶּה.

Ba**ruch** ata Ado**nai** Elo**hey**nu me**lech** ha-o**lam**,
sheheche**ya**nu, v'kiya**ma**nu v'higiy'anu laz**man** hazeh.

© Debbie Friedman

מחזור לחיים

There are three themes of Rosh HaShanah that form the basis for the Shofar Service. They are

Malchuyot: Sovereignty, which Awakens our awe

Zichronot: Memory, we link ourselves through memory to the covenant

Shofarot: The Shofar awakens us to itself.

Tradition teaches that one day God will sound the Great Shofar of Freedom, calling us back from the suffering of alienation and exile.

Malchuyot/Sovereignty

Our prayer room is not this room,
a simple hall wherein we yearly gather for the Days of Awe.

Our prayer room is the most resplendent hall of all the universe,
With ceilings reaching higher than the highest heavens,
Blazing in the light of the candelabra of the sun.

Our prayer room, illumined by the heavens,
Is the throne room of the Sovereign of earth and heaven,
The Monarch more powerful by far than any power we can know.

תְּקִיעָה שְׁבָרִים-תְּרוּעָה תְּקִיעָה

Teki-ah   Shevariym - Teru-ah   Teki-ah

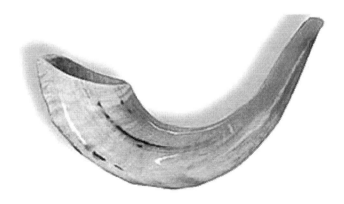

Hayom **ha**rat olam.   הַיּוֹם הֲרַת עוֹלָם.

Today is the birthday of the world. Today, all creatures of the world stand before You as children and as servants. As children, be compassionate with us as a mother or father is with their children. As servants, we look to You with humility and dependence, that You might shine the light of Your justice and power of holiness.

❀❀❀❀❀❀

The expressions of our lips testify before You, mighty and forgiving One, understand, listen, see and grasp fully the voice of our shofar calls; receive with compassion and desire our call to Your sovereignty.

❀❀❀❀❀❀

❀❀❀❀❀❀

Zichronot

❀❀❀❀❀❀

Today is called Yom HaZikaron, "The Day of Remembering".
We start our new year by remembering the year just completed.
What benefit is there in remembering?
> *Do we remember in order to seek recompense?*
> *Do we remember in order to feel guilt?*

No, for we are God's hands and arms and God's heart here on Earth.
Tradition teaches that God moves from a throne of judgement
to a throne of mercy and compassion.
Should we not also be God's image in that way?
> *Let us remember the help from our friends and families.*
> *Let us remember the good people have done for us.*
> *Then we can remember the hurts only long enough to let them go.*

תְּקִיעָה   שְׁבָרִים   תְּקִיעָה

Teki-ah   Shevariym   Teki-ah

❀❀❀❀❀❀

Shofarot

Today we hear the sounding of the Shofar
And it brings everything home to us.
What do we want to keep from last year?
What do we need to release?
Dear God, awaken me to Life!
Dear God, help live it fully!

On the third day, as morning dawned, there were thunderstorms and lightening blasts, and a dense cloud upon the mountain Sinai. We heard the piercing wail of the Shofar and we trembled. The sound of the Shofar grew louder and louder. Moshe spoke and we heard God answer him in claps of thunder. The Shofar cried out as the mountain smoked. We all saw it, and fell back.

When the Temple stood, the Cohanim proclaimed: God has ascended with Teruah! It is God in the sound of the Shofar-blast!

תקיעה תרועה תקיעה

Teki-ah   Teru-ah   Teki-ah

תקיעה גדולה

Teki-ah Gedolah

If you are comfortable doing so, please rise as we open the ark for returning the Torah

עֵץ חַיִּים הִיא לַמַּחֲזִיקִים בָּהּ, וְתֹמְכֶיהָ מְאֻשָּׁר. דְּרָכֶיהָ דַרְכֵי נֹעַם, וְכָל נְתִיבוֹתֶיהָ שָׁלוֹם.

Eitz chayim hi lamachazikiym ba, vetomcheha me-ushar.
Deracheha darchei no-am, vechol netivoteha shalom.
It is a tree of life to those who hold it fast, and all who cling to it find happiness. Its ways are ways of pleasantness, and all its paths are peace.

הֲשִׁיבֵנוּ יְהוָה, אֵלֶיךָ וְנָשׁוּבָה, חַדֵּשׁ יָמֵינוּ כְּקֶדֶם.

Hashiveinu Adonai, eilecha venashuva, chadeish yameinu kekedem.
Help us to return to You, Adonai; then we will return. Renew our days as in the past.
(If you are comfortable doing so, please remain standing for the Aleinu)

❀❀❀❀❀❀

[The ARK is OPENED or remains OPEN after Torah Service]

If you are comfortable doing so, please remain standing or rise as we open the ark for the Aleinu

ADORATION   עָלֵינוּ

עָלֵינוּ לְשַׁבֵּחַ לַאֲדוֹן הַכֹּל, לָתֵת גְּדֻלָה לְיוֹצֵר בְּרֵאשִׁית, שֶׁלֹּא
עָשָׂנוּ עִם גּוֹיֵי הָאֲרָצוֹת, וְלֹא שָׂמָנוּ עִם מִשְׁפְּחוֹת הָאֲדָמָה, שֶׁלֹּא
שָׂם חֶלְקֵנוּ עִמָּהֶם, וְגֹרָלֵנוּ עִם כָּל הָעוֹלָם.
וַאֲנַחְנוּ כּוֹרְעִים וּמִשְׁתַּחֲוִים וּמוֹדִים,
לִפְנֵי מֶלֶךְ, מַלְכֵי הַמְּלָכִים, הַקָּדוֹשׁ בָּרוּךְ הוּא.

Aleinu leshabei-ach la-adon hakol, lateit gedulah l'yotzeir b'reishiyt, shelo
asanu iym goyei ha-aratzot, velo samanu iym mishpechot ha-adamah, shelo
sam chelkeinu imahem, v'goraleinu iym kol ha-olam.
      V'anachnu kor'iym umishtachaviym umodiym.
Lifnei Melech, malchei hamlachiym, haKadosh Baruch Hu.

It is up to us to praise the Source of all, to give due greatness to the One who
created at the very beginning, who gave us a purpose among the nations of the
earth, sending us among the families of the earth, giving us a Divine assignment,
working with all of the world.

      Therefore, we bend our knees, bow, approach and give thanks
before the Ultimate Sovereign, The Holy One, the Source of Blessing.

❀❀❀❀❀❀

Let us adore the ever living God, and render praise unto You,
who spread out the heavens and established the earth,
whose glory is revealed in the heavens above, and whose greatness is manifest
throughout the world. You are our God, there is none else.
We bow the head in reverence and worship
HaKadosh Baruch Hu, the Holy One, Praised be God.
Va-anachnu koriym umishtachaviym umodiym lifnei Melech malchei hamlachiym,
HaKadosh Baruch Hu, the Holy One, Praised be God. Amen.

❀❀❀❀❀❀

(Ark is closed -- Please be seated)

May the time not be distant, O God, when Your name will be worshipped in all the earth, when unbelief will disappear and error be no more.

Fervently we pray that the day may come when all will turn to You in love, when corruption and evil will give way to integrity and goodness, when superstition will no longer enslave the mind, nor idolatry blind the eye, when all who dwell on earth will know that You alone are God. O may all, created in Your image, become one in spirit and one in friendship, forever united in Your service. Then will Your rule be established on earth, and the word of Your prophet fulfilled: the Eternal God will reign for ever and ever.

And then both men and women will be gentle,
And then both women and men will be strong,
And then all will be so varied, rich and free,
And then everywhere will be called Eden once again.

Judy Chicago (adapted)

וְנֶאֱמַר, וְהָיָה יהוה לְמֶלֶךְ עַל כָּל הָאָרֶץ, בַּיוֹם הַהוּא יִהְיֶה יהוה אֶחָד, וּשְׁמוֹ אֶחָד:

V'ne-**emar**, v'ha**ya** Ado**nai** l'**me**lech al kol ha-**aretz**, ba**yom** ha**hu** yiye Ado**nai** e**chad**, ush'**mo** e**chad**.

On that day, O God, You will be One and Your Name will be One.

❈❈❈❈❈❈

קדיש יתום
Mourner's Kaddish

We now ask those of you who are in mourning or who are observing the *Yahrzeit* of a loved one to stand and share their names with us.... Let us support you through the first paragraph and then rise with you. In this way we can link our memories with yours in the hope that we will thus draw strength and comfort from each other. Together we praise God's name.   (English translation on page 5)

יִתְגַּדַּל וְיִתְקַדַּשׁ שְׁמֵהּ רַבָּא. בְּעָלְמָא דִּי בְרָא כִרְעוּתֵיהּ, וְיַמְלִיךְ מַלְכוּתֵיהּ בְּחַיֵּיכוֹן וּבְיוֹמֵיכוֹן וּבְחַיֵּי דְכָל בֵּית יִשְׂרָאֵל. בַּעֲגָלָא וּבִזְמַן קָרִיב וְאִמְרוּ אָמֵן:

Yitga**dal** v'yitka**dash** shi**mei** ra**ba** b'alma di v'ra chiru**tei**, v'yam**lich** malchu**tei** b'chayei**chon** uv'yomei**chon** uv'cha**yei** d'chol beit Yisra-eil, ba-aga**la**, ba-aga**la**, uviz**man** ka**riv**, v'im'ru: A**mein**.

יְהֵא שְׁמֵהּ רַבָּא מְבָרַךְ לְעָלַם וּלְעָלְמֵי עָלְמַיָּא:

Ye**hei** sh'mei **ra**ba m'va**rach** l'**a**lam ul'al**mei** almaya.

יִתְבָּרַךְ וְיִשְׁתַּבַּח וְיִתְפָּאַר וְיִתְרוֹמַם וְיִתְנַשֵּׂא וְיִתְהַדָּר וְיִתְעַלֶּה וְיִתְהַלָּל שְׁמֵהּ דְּקֻדְשָׁא בְּרִיךְ הוּא לְעֵלָּא לְעֵלָּא מִכָּל בִּרְכָתָא וְשִׁירָתָא תֻּשְׁבְּחָתָא וְנֶחֱמָתָא, דַּאֲמִירָן בְּעָלְמָא, וְאִמְרוּ אָמֵן:

Yitba**rach**, v'yishta**bach**, v'yitpa-**ar**, v'yitro**mam**, v'yitna**sei**, v'yit-ha**dar**, v'yit-a**leh**, v'yit-ha**lal** sh'mei d'kud**sha**, brich hu. L'**eila** l'**eila** mi**kol** bircha**ta** v'shira**ta**, tushb'cha**ta** v'nechema**ta** da-ami**ran** b'alma, v'im'ru: Amein.

יְהֵא שְׁלָמָא רַבָּא מִן שְׁמַיָּא, וְחַיִּים עָלֵינוּ וְעַל כָּל יִשְׂרָאֵל וְאִמְרוּ אָמֵן.

Y'**hei** sh'lama **ra**ba min sh'ma**ya**, v'cha**yim** aleinu v'**al** kol Yisra-eil, v'imru: amein.

עֹשֶׂה שָׁלוֹם בִּמְרוֹמָיו הוּא יַעֲשֶׂה שָׁלוֹם עָלֵינוּ וְעַל כָּל יִשְׂרָאֵל, (וְעַל כָּל יוֹשְׁבֵי תֵבֵל,) וְאִמְרוּ אָמֵן:

Oseh sha**lom** bimro**mav**, hu ya-a**seh** sha**lom** aleinu, v'**al** kol Yisra-eil, (v'al kol yosh**vei** tey**veil**,) v'imru: amein.

May the Source of peace send peace to all who mourn and comfort to all who are bereaved in our midst, and let us say, Amen.

❈❈❈❈❈

ADON OLAM

אֲדוֹן עוֹלָם אֲשֶׁר מָלַךְ, בְּטֶרֶם כָּל יְצִיר נִבְרָא.
לְעֵת נַעֲשָׂה בְחֶפְצוֹ כֹּל, אֲזַי מֶלֶךְ שְׁמוֹ נִקְרָא.

Adon Olam, asher Malach beterem kol yetziyr nivra.
l'eit na-asah b'cheftzo kol azai Melech Shemo nikra.

Source of All, who was Sovereign before any forms were created.
At the time of making, it was all through the One's longings. Then, the Name was called out as Sovereign

וְאַחֲרֵי כִּכְלוֹת הַכֹּל, לְבַדּוֹ יִמְלוֹךְ נוֹרָא.
וְהוּא הָיָה, וְהוּא הֹוֶה, וְהוּא יִהְיֶה, בְּתִפְאָרָה.

V'acharei kichlot hakol levado yimloch nora.
V'Hu haya, v'Hu hoveh v'Hu yihyeh, betif'ara.

And afterwards, when all is completed, the One will reign alone through awe
And the One was, and the One is, and the One will be, Splendorous.

וְהוּא אֶחָד וְאֵין שֵׁנִי, לְהַמְשִׁיל לוֹ לְהַחְבִּירָה.
בְּלִי רֵאשִׁית בְּלִי תַכְלִית, וְלוֹ הָעֹז וְהַמִּשְׂרָה.

V'Hu echad v'ein sheini lehamshiyl lo l'hachbirah.
b'liy reishiyt beli tachliyt v'Lo ha-oz vehamisrah.

And the One is one, and never changes, the One reigns, fully joined.
Without beginning, without limit, with Energy and Place.

וְהוּא אֵלִי וְחַי גֹּאֲלִי, וְצוּר חֶבְלִי בְּעֵת צָרָה.
וְהוּא נִסִּי וּמָנוֹס לִי מְנָת כּוֹסִי בְּיוֹם אֶקְרָא.

V'Hu Eiliy v'chai go'ali vetzur chevliy b'eit tzarah.
V'Hu niysiy umanos liy menat kosi beyom ekra.

And the One is my Source, redeeming my life a Rock in my suffering when I am distressed
And the One tempers me and is my refuge, the portion in my cup on the day I am called

בְּיָדוֹ אַפְקִיד רוּחִי, בְּעֵת אִישַׁן וְאָעִירָה.
וְעִם רוּחִי גְּוִיָּתִי, יְהוה לִי וְלֹא אִירָא.

B'yado afkiyd ruchiy b'eit iyshan va-a-iyrah.
V'im ruchiy g'viyatiy Adonai liy velo iyra.

Into the One's hand I entrust my Soul at the time of sleep and arising.
And with my Soul, my body, is for me, I will not fear.

🌸🌸🌸🌸🌸
Meditation

Rabbi Johanan said it in the name of Rabbi Simeon bar Yochai: It is better for a person to cast him or herself into a fiery furnace rather than put another person to shame in public. (B. Talmud, Brachot)
🌸🌸🌸🌸🌸

If you are comfortable doing so,
please join our congregational tradition of standing and moving together, linking arms
with your neighbors as we sing our final service prayer together.

'TFILAT HADERECH"

May we be blessed as we go on our way.
May we be guided in peace.
May we be blessed with health and joy.
May this be our blessing, Amen.

Amen, Amen, may this be our blessing, Amen.

May we be sheltered by the wings of peace.
May we be kept in safety and in love.
May grace and compassion find their way to every soul.
May this be our blessing, Amen.

Amen, Amen, may this be our blessing, Amen.
© Debbie Friedman

L'SHANAH TOVAH TIKATEIVU!!!
(MAY YOU BE INSCRIBED FOR A GOOD YEAR!)

G'MAR CHATIMA TOVA!!!
(MAY YOUR INSCRIPTION FOR A GOOD YEAR BE SEALED!)

Yom Kippur
Service

בְּרֹאשׁ הַשָּׁנָה יִכָּתֵבוּן, וּבְיוֹם צוֹם כִּפּוּר יֵחָתֵמוּן.

BeRosh HaShanah yikateivun. Uv'Yom Tzom Kippur yeichateimun.

On Rosh Hashanah it is written And on Yom Kippur it is sealed:

Yom Kippur Service

מַה טֹּבוּ אֹהָלֶיךָ יַעֲקֹב, מִשְׁכְּנֹתֶיךָ יִשְׂרָאֵל.

Mah **tovu** oha**le**cha Ya-a**kov**, Mishkeno**te**cha Yisra-**eil**.

Blessings flow into the world from the Source of Life.
Be a vessel for the lovesong of God © R. Hanna Tiferet Siegel
How good are your tents Jacob, your in-dwelling places, O Israel.

❀❀❀❀❀

הַלְלוּיָהּ: וַאֲנַחְנוּ נְבָרֵךְ יָהּ, מֵעַתָּה וְעַד עוֹלָם, הַלְלוּיָהּ:

Halelu-**Yahh**; Va-a**nach**nu neva**rech** Yahh, Me'**ata** v'ad o**lam**, Halelu-**Yahh**:

Praise Adonai (Yahh): And we will bless Adonai (Yahh) from now and until eternity, Praise Adonai (Yahh):

❀❀❀❀❀

מַה גָּדְלוּ מַעֲשֶׂיךָ יהוה מְאֹד עָמְקוּ מַחְשְׁבֹתֶיךָ. הַלְלוּיָהּ.

Ma god**lu** ma-a**se**cha Yahh me-**od** am**ku** machshevo**te**cha. (Hallelu**Yahh**)

How great are Your actions, Adonai; Your thoughts are very deep. (HalleluYahh - Praise God)

❀❀❀❀❀

When I sing the Name of God my spirit rises
From the depths she soars in the light

שַׁדַּי, שְׁכִינָה, יהוה צְבָאוֹת, הֲוָיָה, מְקוֹר חַיִּים,
צוּר, מָקוֹם, אֵל עֶלְיוֹן, יָהּ, רוּחַ, אֱלוֹהִים.

Shad**dai** Shechi**na** Ado**nai** Tzeva'**ot** Ha**va**ya M'**kor** Cha**yim**
Tzur Ma**kom** Eyl El**yon** Yahh **Ru**ach Elo**him**. © R. Hanna Tiferet "A Voice Calls"

❀❀❀❀❀

Powerful sun full of radiant light, weave us a web that spins the night.
Web of stars that holds the dark, weave us the earth that feeds the spark.
Strand by strand, hand over hand; Thread by thread, we weave the web.

❀❀❀❀❀

הֲשִׁיבֵנוּ יהוה, אֵלֶיךָ וְנָשׁוּבָה, חַדֵּשׁ יָמֵינוּ כְּקֶדֶם.

Hashi**vei**nu Ado**nai**, ei**le**cha vena**shu**va, cha**deish** ya**mei**nu keke**dem**.

Help us to return to You, Adonai; then we will return. Renew our days as in the past.

❀❀❀❀❀

Bar'chu, Dear One, Shechinah, Holy Name,
When I call on the Light of my Soul, I come home. Lev Friedman

❀❀❀❀❀

We are opening up in sweet surrender to the luminous lovelight
of the One. We are opening.

❀❀❀❀❀

※※※※※

Nish-ma-**ti** a-hu-**vah** le-hit-cha-**reit** ha-kli-**pah**
le-tshu-**vah** u-sli-**chah**
le-to-**dah** u-vra-**chah** Halelluh**Yahh**, Halelluh**Yahh**

נִשְׁמָתִי אֲהוּבָה
לְהִתְחָרֵט הַקְּלִיפָּה
לִתְשׁוּבָה וּסְלִיחָה
לְתוֹדָה וּבְרָכָה
הַלְלוּיָהּ הַלְלוּיָהּ

O my Soul, I Love You,
Pain and Sorrow from my life, Repenting and Releasing
Thanks to You, Blessings come
HalelluhYahh   HalelluhYahh

※※※※※

Meditation

טז רְאֵה נָתַתִּי לְפָנֶיךָ הַיּוֹם אֶת־הַחַיִּים וְאֶת־הַטּוֹב וְאֶת־הַמָּוֶת וְאֶת־הָרָע:
יט ... הַעִדֹתִי בָכֶם הַיּוֹם אֶת־הַשָּׁמַיִם וְאֶת־הָאָרֶץ הַחַיִּים וְהַמָּוֶת נָתַתִּי
לְפָנֶיךָ הַבְּרָכָה וְהַקְּלָלָה וּבָחַרְתָּ בַּחַיִּים לְמַעַן תִּחְיֶה אַתָּה וְזַרְעֶךָ:

R'**ei** na**ta**ti l'**fa**necha ha**yom** et hacha**yiym** v'**et** ha**tov** v'**et** ha**ma**vet v'**et** hara'. ...
ha'i**do**ti va**chem** ha**yom** et hasha**ma**yim v'**et** ha-**a**retz, hacha**yiym** veha**ma**vet na**ta**ti
l'**fa**necha habra**cha** vehak**la**la uva**char**ta bacha**yiym** lema-**an** tih**yeh** a**ta** veza**re**cha.
Understand, I have placed before you today life and goodness and death and
wickedness. ... I make witnesses today of the heavens and the earth that life and death I
have placed before you, the blessing and the the curse; choose life so that you and your
generations will live. (Deut 30:15,19)

※※※※※

God - What is today about? Every day I wrestle with You.
How can You love me when I do that?

> God, every day I long to feel Your Presence within me.
> How do I make that happen?

God, this is a complex world You have made for us,
Full of interconnections and invisible strings.
God, I do not even know how to pronounce Your holy name,
What would happen if we managed to speak Your holy name?
Would the hurt and tragedy stop?
It never stopped for Jacob, even when he became Israel
And even Moses struggled with anger to the very end.

> What is it about You that created the world the way it is?
> Is it blasphemy to question You this way?
> Jacob struggled all night long and he prevailed.
> Will we prevail?
> Help us deal kindly with ourselves and with each other.
> Help us to forgive and to seek forgiveness with an open heart.

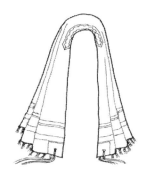

בָּרוּךְ אַתָּה יהוה אֱלֹהֵינוּ מֶלֶךְ הָעוֹלָם אֲשֶׁר קִדְּשָׁנוּ בְּמִצְוֹתָיו, וְצִוָּנוּ לְהִתְעַטֵּף בַּצִּיצִת.

Baruch ata Adonai Eloheinu melech ha-olam, asher kidshanu b'mitzvotav, vetzivanu, lehitateif batzitzit.

The Source of Blessing are You, Eternal Sovereign. You make us special with Mitzvot and instruct us to enwrap ourself with tzitzit (tallit).

Meditation

If one says, I will sin and Yom Kippur will atone for it, Yom Kippur does not atone. For transgressions against the Holy One, Yom Kippur atones. For transgressions between individuals, Yom Kippur does not atone until one sets things right with the one harmed. (Mishna Yoma 8:9)

God, the time has come again for us to invoke Your heavenly court.
In Torah, You told us that Heaven and Earth would be witnesses
against us in our shortfalls and that the Torah itself would be our counsel.

> *And so we call on that court now. We call on heaven and earth and the Torah.*
> *May they form Your court that we might invoke them.*

In some congregations that court is represented by three Torah scrolls.
In some congregations it is represented by one scroll and two people.
In other congregations it is represented by three people.

עֵץ חַיִּים הִיא לַמַּחֲזִיקִים בָּהּ, וְתוֹמְכֶיהָ מְאֻשָּׁר. דְּרָכֶיהָ דַרְכֵי נוֹעַם, וְכָל נְתִיבוֹתֶיהָ שָׁלוֹם.

Eitz chayim hi lamachazikiym ba, vetomche-ah me-ushar. Derache-ah darchei no-am, vechol netivote-ah shalom.

It is a tree of life to those who hold it fast, and all who cling to it find happiness. Its ways are ways of pleasantness, and all its paths are peace.

We have come to hear, and thereby be part of, Kol Nidre.

> *Kol Nidre is a paradox because life itself is a paradox.*
> *Kol Nidre, is not a prayer at all.*
> *It is a legal formula nullifying and cancelling all our vows.*
> *Not those between people, only those between a person and God.*
> *But this is the greatest paradox of all, the human paradox:*
> *We need to vow, to swear commitment to future hopes, to higher ideals,*

Knowing that our reach exceeds our grasp
And that some of our vows will be made in vain.
Nevertheless we pray:

> *All vows, promises, and commitments we made since last*
> *Yom Kippur and in the years before - May we be given strength to keep them.*

Our marriage vows - may they endure;
Our vows for good health, to exercise, to diet;
The promises we made to study and to worship;
Commitments to parents and to friends,
pledges to charity, and to work for others.

> *Help us be as compassionate and generous as we felt*
> *ourselves to be at those moments.*

O God, sometimes I feel rotten inside. I feel empty, phony.
And no one else knows how bad I feel.

> *They think I am fine ... doing well ... successful even.*
> *But I know all the times I have failed.*

The resolutions from last Rosh Hashanah faded away so quickly.
My bad habits ... remain unbroken.
My good intentions ... remain unrealized.

> *There are no new vows I can make ... no new efforts to push, I give up.*

And then, during the Kol Nidre, I hear your plea, "Get up!
I only commanded one day for afflicting your soul.
I gave you ten days for repentance,
For turning over a new leaf in the Book of Life.
Even if you don't have faith in yourself I have faith in you.
Get up off the floor and get up quickly
Falling isn't the worst sin, staying on the floor is."

כָּל נִדְרֵי וֶאֱסָרֵי וַחֲרָמֵי, וְקוֹנָמֵי וְכִנּוּיֵי, וְקִנּוּסֵי וּשְׁבוּעוֹת, דִּנְדַרְנָא
וּדְאִשְׁתַּבַּעְנָא, וּדְאַחֲרֶמְנָא וְדִאֲסַרְנָא עַל נַפְשָׁתָנָא, מִיּוֹם כִּפֻּרִים זֶה
עַד יוֹם כִּפֻּרִים הַבָּא עָלֵינוּ לְטוֹבָה, כֻּלְּהוֹן אִחֲרַטְנָא בְהוֹן. כֻּלְּהוֹן
יְהוֹן שָׁרָן, שְׁבִיקִין שְׁבִיתִין, בְּטֵלִין וּמְבֻטָּלִין, לָא שְׁרִירִין וְלָא קַיָּמִין.
נִדְרָנָא לָא נִדְרֵי, וֶאֱסָרָנָא לָא אֱסָרֵי, וּשְׁבוּעָתָנָא לָא שְׁבוּעוֹת.

Kol nidrei, ve-esarei vacharamei, vekonamei, vechinuyei, vekinusei ushvu-ot, dindarna ude-ishtaba'na, ude-achareimna vedi-asarna al nafshatana, miyom kipuriym ze ad yom kipuriym haba aleinu letovah, kulhon icharatna vehon. Kulhon yehon sharan, sheviykiyn sheviytiyn, beteiliyn umvutaliyn, la sheriyriyn vela kayamiyn. Nidrana la nidrei, ve-esarana la esarei, ushvu'atana la shevu'ot.

All vows, bonds of abstinence, boycotts, sacraments, promises, obligations, and oaths [to God], that we vow and that we swear and that we utter and all that we forbid ourselves regarding our souls, from this day of Yom Kippur until the next Yom Kippur, that we undertake [with God] for our welfare, for all of these, we do repent. [God,] All of them are to be dissolved, releasing and released, cancelled and annulled, not valid and not established. Our vows [to You] are not to be considered vows, our bonds of abstinence [to You] are not bonds and our oaths [to You] are not oaths.

וְנִסְלַח לְכָל עֲדַת בְּנֵי יִשְׂרָאֵל וְלַגֵּר הַגָּר בְּתוֹכָם, כִּי לְכָל הָעָם בִּשְׁגָגָה.

Venislach lechol 'adat benei Yisra-eil velageir hagar betocham, ki lechol ha'am bishgagah.

And all of the community of Israel will be pardoned as well as the stranger in their midst, because the whole people err [in doing such things].

סְלַח נָא לַעֲוֹן הָעָם הַזֶּה כְּגֹדֶל חַסְדֶּךָ, וְכַאֲשֶׁר נָשָׂאתָה לָעָם הַזֶּה מִמִּצְרַיִם וְעַד הֵנָּה. וְשָׁם נֶאֱמַר: וַיֹּאמֶר יהוה סָלַחְתִּי כִּדְבָרֶךָ.

Selach na la'avon ha'am hazeh kegodel chasdecha, vecha-asher nasata la'am hazeh miMitzrayim ve'ad heina. Vesham ne-emar: vayomer Adonai salachtiy kidvarecha.

Please forgive the transgressions of this people because Your mercy is great and thus You have carried and pardoned and forgiven this people even from Egypt and even to the here and now, as it is written:
"And Adonai said, I forgive them as I have spoken." (Num 14:20)

If you are more comfortable sitting, please do so at this time or at any time.

Today we stand before You to affirm our faith in the Holy One, to God for giving us life, for sustaining us, and for enabling us to reach this season. Amen!

בָּרוּךְ אַתָּה יהוה אֱלֹהֵינוּ מֶלֶךְ הָעוֹלָם,

שֶׁהֶחֱיָנוּ וְקִיְּמָנוּ וְהִגִּיעָנוּ לַזְּמַן הַזֶּה.

Baruch **ata** Ado**nai** Elo**hei**nu **me**lech ha-**o**lam,
shehoche**ya**nu, v'kiye**ma**nu v'higiy'**a**nu laz**man** ha**zeh.**
The Source of Blessing are You, Eternal Sovereign.
You give us life, You sustain us and You bring us to this Time.

הוֹדוּ לַיהוה כִּי טוֹב, כִּי לְעוֹלָם חַסְדּוֹ:

יֹאמַר־נָא יִשְׂרָאֵל כִּי לְעוֹלָם חַסְדּוֹ:

Hodu la'Ado**nai** ki tov, ki l'**o**lam chas**do**:
Yomar-na Yisra-**eil**, ki l'**o**lam chas**do**:

Let all who revere God's Name now say, "Ki l'olam chasdo"
Sing praise to the One for God is good, ki l'olam chasdo.
Give thanks to Adonai for God is good and God's mercy endures forever.
Say it, please, Israel for God's mercy endures forever. Ps 118:1-2

CHATZI KADDISH　　　חצי קדיש

יִתְגַּדַּל וְיִתְקַדַּשׁ שְׁמֵהּ רַבָּא. בְּעָלְמָא דִּי בְרָא כִרְעוּתֵהּ,

וְיַמְלִיךְ מַלְכוּתֵהּ בְּחַיֵּיכוֹן וּבְיוֹמֵיכוֹן וּבְחַיֵּי דְכָל בֵּית יִשְׂרָאֵל.

בַּעֲגָלָא וּבִזְמַן קָרִיב וְאִמְרוּ אָמֵן:

יְהֵא שְׁמֵהּ רַבָּא מְבָרַךְ לְעָלַם וּלְעָלְמֵי עָלְמַיָּא:

יִתְבָּרַךְ וְיִשְׁתַּבַּח, וְיִתְפָּאַר וְיִתְרוֹמַם וְיִתְנַשֵּׂא וְיִתְהַדָּר וְיִתְעַלֶּה

וְיִתְהַלָּל שְׁמֵהּ דְּקֻדְשָׁא בְּרִיךְ הוּא לְעֵלָּא לְעֵלָּא מִכָּל בִּרְכָתָא

וְשִׁירָתָא, תֻּשְׁבְּחָתָא וְנֶחֱמָתָא, דַּאֲמִירָן בְּעָלְמָא, וְאִמְרוּ אָמֵן:

Yitgadal v'yitka**dash** shi**mei** raba b'**al**ma di v'ra chiru**tei**, v'yam**lich** malchu**tei**
b'chayei**chon** uv'yomei**chon** uv'cha**yei** d'chol beit Yisra-**eil**, ba-a**ga**la, ba-a**ga**la,
uviz**man** ka**riv**, v'im'**ru**: A**mein**.
Ye**hei** sh'mei ra**ba** m'va**rach** l'**alam** ul'al**mei** al**maya**.
Yitba**rach**, v'yishta**bach**, v'yitpa-**ar**, v'yitro**mam**, v'yitna**sei**, v'yit-ha**dar**, v'yit-a**leh**,
v'yit-ha**lal** sh'mei d'kud**sha**, brich hu. L'**ei**la l'**ei**la mi**kol** bircha**ta** v'shira**ta**, tushb'**cha**ta
v'nechema**ta** da-ami**ran** b'**al**ma, v'im'**ru**: Amein.

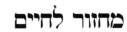

Let God's gloriousness be extolled, God's great Name be hallowed in the world whose creation God willed. And may God's reign be in our day, during our life, and the life of all Israel, and let us say: Amen.

Let God's great Name be praised forever and ever.

Let the Name of the Holy One, the Blessing One, be glorified, exalted, and honored, though God is beyond all the praises, songs, and adorations that we can utter, and let us say: Amen.

Dear One of Many Names,

I need to call out to you again today.
I've been talking to others about the hurts we all feel and I still feel
Like I'm the one who has come out on the short end of the deal.

Is it so wrong to want things my way?
Is it so wrong to demand to know all the ins and outs of the things
I care about or that might affect me?

The haunting melody of the Kol Nidre still echoes in my ears.
Help me face myself tonight and through the coming year, Compassionate One.

Help us hold our tempers when they seek to flare,
Help us be strong when others need some help,
Help us have enough to give when so much is needed.

Help us to be wise and thoughtful and think things through,
Help us to see the good where ever it may surface,
Help us to remember that life is Your precious gift.

If I really work at recognizing my own failings, can I make a fresh start?
We come together to support each other in our quest
In our joint questing, perhaps we can find the safety we need
from and with each other.

May we find the safety and the comfort we need to visit our own hurting places
So that we can see the hurt we have inflicted on others and on our selves.
When we can do that, we are doing the work we need to do this Yom Kippur.

Then maybe we can say "I'm sorry" and mean it.
Maybe then we can hear the repentance in our friends and loved ones.
And know that they, too, mean it.

Maybe we will remember to live every day as if it were our last.
May we feel Your Presence and acknowledge it every day,
May we help others see Your Presence in how we live every day.

MA TOVU

מה טבו

מַה טֹּבוּ אֹהָלֶיךָ יַעֲקֹב, מִשְׁכְּנֹתֶיךָ יִשְׂרָאֵל.
וַאֲנִי בְּרֹב חַסְדְּךָ אָבוֹא בֵיתֶךָ,
אֶשְׁתַּחֲוֶה אֶל הֵיכַל קָדְשְׁךָ בְּיִרְאָתֶךָ.

Mah tovu ohalecha Ya-akov, Mishkenotecha Yisra-eil.
Va-ani berov chasdecha avo veytecha
Eshtachaveh el heychal kodshecha b'yiratecha.

O how good are your tents, Jacob, your dwelling-places, Israel.
And I, through Your abundant loving kindness, now enter Your House,
drawing near, seeking You, in the house of Your holiness.

Mah tovu ohalecha Ya-akov, Mishkenotecha Yisra-eil.
Blessings flow into the world from the Source of Life.
Be a vessel for the lovesong of God © R. Hanna Tiferet Siegel

Prayer is something we do for ourselves, to calm us,
to give ourselves quiet, confidence and inner peace.
> *We come here to probe our weaknesses and our strengths,*
> *To bridge the gap between what we claim and what we are.*

Prayer helps us see beyond the illusions of success and self
fulfillment
Of individualism and independence that feed the ego and not the person.
> *We come here to quiet the turbulence within our hearts,*
> *To curb our desires to best one another, to out-smart or out-distance each other.*

May we find in our prayers the beauty of coming together as community,
to supporting each other and our faith and our faith in life.

הִנֵּה מַה טּוֹב וּמַה נָּעִים שֶׁבֶת אַחִים גַּם יָחַד.
Hinei ma tov umah na-iym shevet achiym gam yachad.
Behold how good and how pleasant it is when brethren dwell together.

הַלְלוּהוּ בְּצִלְצְלֵי שָׁמַע, הַלְלוּהוּ בְּצִלְצְלֵי תְרוּעָה:
כֹּל הַנְּשָׁמָה תְּהַלֵּל יָהּ הַלְלוּיָהּ.

Haleluhu betziltzelei shama. Haleluhu betziltzelei tru'ah.
Kol hanshamah tehaleil Yahh, HaleluYahh.
Praise the Source with crashing cymbals! Praise the Source with resounding voice!
Let all who breathe now praise their Source! Hallelujah (Praise Yahh)! (Psalm 150)

נִשְׁמַת כָּל חַי, תְּבָרֵךְ אֶת שִׁמְךָ יהוה אֱלֹהֵינוּ.

Nish**mat** kol chai, teva**reich** et shim**cha** (Yahh or Ado**nai**) Elo**hei**nu.
The breath of all life, Praises You, (Yahh or Adonai) our God.

Sho**chein**, sho**chein** ad
Ma**rom** veka**dosh** She**mo**
vecha**tuv**, ka**dosh** She**mo**...
Sho**chein**...

שׁוֹכֵן שׁוֹכֵן עַד,
מָרוֹם וְקָדוֹשׁ שְׁמוֹ:
וְכָתוּב, קָדוֹשׁ שְׁמוֹ ...... שׁוֹכֵן...

You dwell within, for all time
Exalted, sacred are You
It is written, Sacred are You... Sho**chein**...

The righteous rejoice in You
The upright seek Your glory
It is written, Sacred are You... Sho**chein**...

God, the time has come again for me to do the hardest work I can do,
working on my Self. I need Your help if I am to be able to do it well.

Help me face questions I wish to avoid!
Help me accept truths which do not comfort!
I wish to journey to the light, but the path is hidden
by all of the promises I never kept, by the goodness I forgot.

The gates of prayer are sometimes open and sometimes closed,
while the gates of repentance are always open.
The Holy One's hand is always open to receive penitents.
When we see You are our Sovereign and are the truly ultimate power
and that You wield Your power with love and compassion,
it becomes easier to reach out our hands to You.

הַמֶּלֶךְ

הַיּוֹשֵׁב עַל כִּסֵּא רָם וְנִשָּׂא:

Ha**Me**lech -- hayo**sheiv** al ki**sei** ram v'ni**sa**.
The Sovereign, who dwells enthroned, high and exalted.

Today the song is ours. We rejoice and we shout.

The world is bright yellow and flashing green.
Miracles surround us all around.

Today, we can believe in miracles.
We can find at least one leaf or one flower for which to thank you.

Praise God, O my Soul. Sing out God's praises now.
From my innermost depths to my loftiest heights, let me praise You.

If you are comfortable doing so, please rise and let us sing the 'BAR'CHU'

Bar'**chu** et A**do**nai ham'vo**rach**.   בָּרְכוּ אֶת יהוה הַמְבֹרָךְ:

We praise Adonai, the Source of Blessing, Who blesses.

בָּרוּךְ יהוה הַמְבֹרָךְ לְעוֹלָם וָעֶד:
Ba**ruch** A**do**nai hamevo**rach** l'**olam** va'**ed**.
Praised be Adonai, the Source of Blessing, now and forever.

Bar'chu, Dear One, Shechinah, Holy Name,
When I call on the Light of my Soul, I come home.
Lev Friedman

Praise the One to whom all praise is due.
Praised be the One to whom all praise is due, Now and forever.
Praise the One to whom all praise is due.
Praised be the One to whom all praise is due
Now and forever, now and forever, now and forever, praise the One.

We are seated

You are to be praised
Who rolls out the rough, raw clay of the universe
Into delicate vessels of light,
And from nothing at all
Creates the darkness which lets them shine.
Your vessels pour light upon the universe
Flooding the cracks in our darkness with the beams of Your compassion.

You are Praised
Who forms from the clay that cloaks our lives,
The delicate vessels
which are our light.

Baruch Ata, Adonai

Eloheinu melech ha-Olam,

yotzeir or, uvorei choshech,

oseh shalom uvorei et hakol.

Baruch Ata Adonai,

yotzeir ham'orot.

בָּרוּךְ אַתָּה יְהֹוָה,

אֱלֹהֵינוּ מֶלֶךְ הָעוֹלָם,

יוֹצֵר אוֹר, וּבוֹרֵא חֹשֶׁךְ,

עֹשֶׂה שָׁלוֹם וּבוֹרֵא אֶת הַכֹּל.

בָּרוּךְ אַתָּה יְהֹוָה,

יוֹצֵר הַמְּאוֹרוֹת:

A Source of Blessing are You, Adonai, our God, Sovereign of the universe, who forms light and creates darkness, makes peace and creates everything. A Source of Blessing are You, Adonai, our God, Sovereign of the universe, who forms the lights.

I am confused, God. Is it our times, our world, our society?
Or is it, dear God, only me?

> *There are times when I feel pulled apart.*
> *I have so many responsibilities -*
> *Have I given my family enough of myself,*

Or have I too often asked them to wait?
I have tried to be present, to be concerned,
Compassionate, understanding, loving;

> *If I have failed them*
> *Then let me know the purpose of that failure.*

For their hurts are my hurts, their simchas are my joys,
Their growth is my growth, their wisdom is my wisdom.
O Holy One of Israel, bless my loved ones, keep them wise and strong.

> *My hopes and dreams are in front of me, Your Love surrounds me.*

Sometimes it is easier to say "I'm sorry" than to accept it if someone hurts me.
Do they think that "I'm sorry" erases the pain?
Is "I'm sorry" enough to restore my well-being?

   It is often easier to ask forgiveness than to forgive.

Yet what do I mean when I say "I'm sorry?"
Is it merely a way to smoothen an awkward moment,
To relieve my own anxieties with a formal phrase?

   Perhaps I say my own "I'm sorry"s too easily
   And so I suspect that others do the same.

If I become more committed to my own "I'm sorry"s
I might more readily believe that others are committed to theirs.

   Sometimes I withhold forgiveness as a means of punishment,
   Exercising power over a friend, taking revenge by nursing my hurt inside.

But by withholding "I forgive you,"
I really myself back from the very people whose caring could alleviate my pain.

   For how can other people really hurt me or shoot holes in my well-being?
   I may not be prepared for their remarks,

I may suddenly feel that my friend is not so good a friend, so let me ask myself:
What leads me to cause another's hurt?
Do I mean to? Not too often.

   Mostly I speak a hurtful word out of my own uncertainty,
   When I feel threatened or belittled.

Not to wound another, just to shore up my own defenses. Do they also hurt?
   Perhaps if I listen to the person behind the remark and be vulnerable
   I can ease their pain and protect my own well-being.

   To forgive readily helps others and it makes me feel whole as well.

Yom Kippur

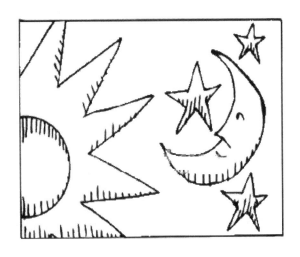

Meditation

WE REACH IN THREE DIRECTIONS

A person reaches in three directions:
Inward, to oneself
Up, to the Eternal One
Out, to others

The miracle of life
Is that in truly reaching in any one direction,
one embraces all three.

Rabbi Nachman of Bretzlov

אַהֲבָה רַבָּה אֲהַבְתָּנוּ, יהוה אֱלֹהֵינוּ, חֶמְלָה גְדוֹלָה וִיתֵרָה חָמַלְתָּ עָלֵינוּ.

Ahava raba ahavtanu Adonai Eloheinu, chemla g'dola viyteira chamalta aleinu.
With abundant love have you loved us, Adonai, our God. With the greatest compassion have you been compassionate to us. Avinu Malkeinu, for the sake of our ancestors who trusted in You and whom You taught the mysteries of life, may You be so gracious to us and teach us. Our Parent, merciful Parent, Who is compassionate, be compassionate with us, instill in our hearts understanding and wisdom, to listen, learn, teach, safeguard, perform, and fulfill all the words of Your Torah's teaching with love.

Meditation

To the glass of water, it makes no difference if one is an optimist or a pessimist.
To a human being, it makes all of the difference in the world.
At any time, in any place, each of us makes that choice.

Bring us in to peacefulness from the four corners of the earth and grant us independence in our land. And bring us close to You with truth to thank You and proclaim Your Oneness with love.

בָּרוּךְ אַתָּה יהוה, אוֹהֵב עַמּוֹ יִשְׂרָאֵל.

Baruch ata Adonai, oheiv amo Yisra-eil.
A Source of Blessing are You, who loves Your people Israel.

To Life! High Holy Day Prayer Book מחזור לחיים

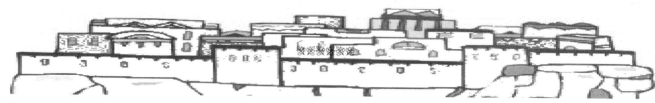

Open to me; open your (my) heart; Let my (Your) Presence dwell in you (me).
I am (You are) within you (me), all around you (me), I (You) fill the universe.

❋❋❋❋❋

The day's light shines and the time is right now.

Help me dig into the earth of my soul.
Please grant me the courage to change, to grow,
to break through the crust of hard soil, of hardened soul.

We have one more chance today to say, "I am sorry."
We have one more chance to do this very hard action.

And unless we find a way to change,
we are trapped forever in yesterday's ways.

Adonai, help us change our ways -
From callousness to sensitivity,
From hostility to love,
From pettiness to purpose,
From envy to contentment,
From carelessness to discipline,
From fear to faith.

❋❋❋❋❋

We are opening up in sweet surrender to the luminous love-light of the One
We are opening.

❋❋❋❋❋

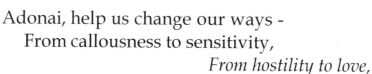

אַשְׁרֵינוּ, מַה טוֹב חֶלְקֵנוּ, וּמַה נָּעִים גוֹרָלֵנוּ, וּמַה יָּפָה יְרֻשָׁתֵנוּ.
אַשְׁרֵינוּ, שֶׁאֲנַחְנוּ וְאוֹמְרִים בְּכָל יוֹם:

Ashreinu, mah tov chelkeinu, umah na-iym goraleinu, umah yafa yerushateinu.
Ashreinu, she-anachnu ve-omriym bechol yom.

Happy are we, how good is our lot, and how pleasant is our fate, and how lovely is our inheritance.
Happy are we, that we say every day:

❋❋❋❋❋

שְׁמַע יִשְׂרָאֵל, יהוה אֱלֹהֵינוּ, יהוה אֶחָד:

Sh'ma Yisra-**eil**: Ado**nai** Elo**hei**nu, Ado**nai Ech**ad!

Hear, O Israel: Adonai is our God, Adonai is One!

(with full voice)

בָּרוּךְ שֵׁם כְּבוֹד מַלְכוּתוֹ לְעוֹלָם וָעֶד.

Baruch sheim ke**vod** male**chu**to le-**olam** va-**ed**!

Blessed is God's glorious majesty for ever and ever!

❀❀❀❀❀

וְאָהַבְתָּ אֵת יהוה אֱלֹהֶיךָ בְּכָל־לְבָבְךָ וּבְכָל־נַפְשְׁךָ וּבְכָל־מְאֹדֶךָ:
וְהָיוּ הַדְּבָרִים הָאֵלֶּה אֲשֶׁר אָנֹכִי מְצַוְּךָ הַיּוֹם עַל־לְבָבֶךָ: וְשִׁנַּנְתָּם
לְבָנֶיךָ וְדִבַּרְתָּ בָּם בְּשִׁבְתְּךָ בְּבֵיתֶךָ וּבְלֶכְתְּךָ בַדֶּרֶךְ וּבְשָׁכְבְּךָ
וּבְקוּמֶךָ: וּקְשַׁרְתָּם לְאוֹת עַל־יָדֶךָ וְהָיוּ לְטֹטָפֹת בֵּין עֵינֶיךָ:
וּכְתַבְתָּם עַל־מְזֻזֹת בֵּיתֶךָ וּבִשְׁעָרֶיךָ:

V'ahav**ta** eit Ado**nai** Elo**he**cha; be**chol** lev**av**cha uv'**chol** nafshe**cha** uve**chol** m'ode**cha**. V'ha**yu** had'va**riym** ha'**ei**leh a**sher** Ano**chi** m'tzav**cha** ha**yom** al leva**ve**cha. V'shinan**tam** l'vane**cha** v'dibar'**ta** bam; b'shiv'te**cha** b'vei**te**cha uv'lechte**cha** vade**rech** uv'shochbe**cha** uvku**me**cha. Ukshar**tam** l'**ot** 'al ya**de**cha; v'ha**yu** l'tota**fot** bein 'eine**cha**. Uchtav**tam** 'al-mezu**zot** bei**te**cha uvish'a**re**cha. (Deut 6:4-9)

❀❀❀❀❀

And thou shalt love the Lord thy God with all of thy heart, with all thy soul, with all of thy might. And all these words which I command ye on this day will be in thy heart. And thou shalt teach them diligently unto thy children. And thou shalt speak of them when thou sittest in thy house, when thou walkest by the way, and when thou risest up and when thou liest down. And thou shalt bind them for a sign upon thy hand. And they shall be for frontlets between thine eyes. And thou shalt bind them on the door posts of thy house, and upon thy gates. That ye may remember and do all of my commandments and be holy unto thy God.

❀❀❀❀❀

וְאָהַבְתָּ אֵת יהוה אֱלֹהֶיךָ בְּכָל לְבָבְךָ וּבְכָל נַפְשְׁךָ וּבְכָל מְאֹדֶךָ:

V'ahav**ta** eit Ado**nai** Elo**he**cha; be**chol** le**vav**cha uv'**chol** nafshe**cha** uve**chol** m'o**de**cha.

And you will teach your children as you live each day.
The path you walk, the way you talk,
And how you listen for the Good in each soul saying...

וְאָהַבְתָּ אֵת יהוה אֱלֹהֶיךָ

Plant seeds of loving kindness in the fertile soil of faith,
The joy we sow will help us grow
A fragrant Garden of Truth embracing...

וְאָהַבְתָּ אֵת יהוה אֱלֹהֶיךָ

We inscribe these words on the door posts of our being
With heart and mind, we each can find
The precious Light that we are seeking...

וְאָהַבְתָּ אֵת יהוה אֱלֹהֶיךָ

We are all God's children, Living on Mother Earth.
Let hatred cease, bless her with peace.
Become the Mountain, Witness, Holy Wonder birthing...

וְאָהַבְתָּ אֵת יהוה אֱלֹהֶיךָ

© R. Hanna Tiferet

Shema Yisrael

Listen! you Yisrael person
יהוה who is, is our God.

יהוה who is, is One,
unique, all there is.

Through Time and Space
Your Glory Shines Majestic One!

Love, that יהוה who is your God,
in what your heart is in,
in what you aspire to,
in what you have made your own.

May these values
which I connect with your life
be implanted in your feelings.

May they become
the norm for your children,
addressing them
in the privacy of your home,
on the errands you run.

May they help you relax,
and activate you to be productive.

Display them visibly on your arm.
Let them focus your attention.
See them in all transitions,
at home and in your environment.

How good it will be
when you really listen
and hear My directions
which I give you today,
for loving יהוה who is your God,
and acting Godly
with feeling and inspiration.

Your earthly needs will be met
at the right time,
appropriate to the season.
You will reap what you have planted
for your delight and health.

And your animals will have ample feed.
All of you will eat and be content.

Be careful -- watch out!
Don't let your cravings delude you.
Don't become alienated.
Don't let your cravings
become your gods.
Don't debase yourself to them,
because the God-sense within you
will become distorted.
Heaven will be shut to you.
Grace will not descend.
Earth will not produce.
Your rushing will destroy you
and Earth will not be able
to recover her good balance
in which God's gifts manifest.

May these values of Mine
reside in your aspirations
marking what you produce,
guiding what you perceive.

Teach them to your children,
so that they be addressed by them
in making their homes,
how they deal with traffic;
when you are depressed
when you are elated.

Mark your entrances and exits
with them so you are more aware.

Then you and your children
will live out on earth
that divine promise
given to your ancestors

to live heavenly days
right here on this earth.

יהוה who is, said to Moshe
"Speak, telling the Israel folks
to make tzitzit
on the corners of their garments
so they will have
generations to follow them.

On each tzitzit-tassel
let them set a blue thread.
Glance at it,
and in your seeing,
remember all the other directives
of יהוה who is, and act on them.

This way you will not be led astray,
craving to see and want,
and then prostitute yourself
for your cravings.

This way you will be mindful
to actualize My directions
for becoming
dedicated to your God,
to be aware that
I AM
יהוה who is your God --
the One who freed you
from the oppression
in order to God you.

I am יהוה your God."
That is the truth.

Interpretive translation by
Reb Zalman Schachter-Shalomi

יְהוָה אֱלֹהֵיכֶם: אֱמֶת..   Adonai Eloheichem. Emet..

אֱמֶת וְיַצִּיב וְנָכוֹן וְקַיָּם וְיָשָׁר וְנֶאֱמָן וְאָהוּב וְחָבִיב וְנֶחְמָד וְנָעִים וְנוֹרָא
וְאַדִּיר וּמְתֻקָּן וּמְקֻבָּל וְטוֹב וְיָפֶה הַדָּבָר הַזֶּה עָלֵינוּ לְעוֹלָם וָעֶד.

Emet ve-yatziv venachon vekayam v'yashar v'ne-eman v'ahuv v'chaviyv v'nechmad
v'na-iym v'nora v'adir umtukan umkubal v'tov v'yafeh hadavar hazeh aleinu le-olam va-ed

True and established, and correct, and upright, and faithful, and beloved, and adored, and desired, and pleasant, and
awesome, and mighty, and powerful, and receiving, and good, and beautiful, is this principal for us forever.

Long ago, Moshe and Miriam had a choice
They could stay in Egypt, the tight place
Where they knew the routine and what was expected of them,
Or they could make a change in their lives and the world.

> *Our ancestors had to choose between sure destruction*
> *from the advancing Egyptian army they were facing*
> *and the impassable sea of water behind them.*
> *They asked the question of where should they turn and saw no answer.*

Moshe turned to God and God said, "Why are you crying to me?
Speak to the Children of Israel and they will move forward."
God explained that Moshe already had the power to split the sea;
it was in his hand in the form of a rod.

> *And so Moshe turned us around that we might see the miracle,*
> *The parting of the sea, the path to freedom and birth,*
> *the path to our own self-determination*
> *To the freedom of being responsible for our own actions.*

And so we journeyed forward into the freedom of responsibility
and the responsibility of freedom.
And we did so on dry ground, safely,
even though danger was on both sides, close enough to touch.

> *May we turn around now and see the miracles around us,*
> *May we find the path to freedom and responsibility*
> *May we see the danger around us and not succumb*
> *May we join with Moshe and Miriam in their song to God.*

Mi cha**mo**cha ba-ei**lim**, Ado**nai**?
Mi ka**mo**cha, ne**dar** ba**ko**desh, no**ra** tehi**lot**, o**sei** fe**leh**?
Shira chada**sha** shib**chu** g'u**liym** l'shim**cha** al sfat ha**yam**, **ya**chad ku**lam** ho**du** v'him**liy**chu v'am**ru**:
"Ado**nai** yim**loch** le-o**lam** va-**ed**"
Tzur Yisra-**eil**, **ku**ma b'ez**rat** Yisra-**eil** uf**dei** chinu**me**cha Yehu**da** v'Yisra-**eil**. Go-a**lei**nu Ado**nai** Tz'va-**ot** She**mo**, Ke**dosh** Yisra-**eil**.
Ba**ruch** A**ta** Ado**nai**, ga-**al** Yisra-**eil** ame**cha**. (chorus)

מִי כָמֹכָה בָּאֵלִים יהוה?
מִי כָּמֹכָה נֶאְדָּר בַּקֹּדֶשׁ,
נוֹרָא תְהִלֹת, עֹשֵׂה פֶלֶא?
שִׁירָה חֲדָשָׁה שִׁבְּחוּ גְאוּלִים לְשִׁמְךָ עַל
שְׂפַת הַיָּם, יַחַד כֻּלָּם הוֹדוּ וְהִמְלִיכוּ
וְאָמְרוּ:
יהוה יִמְלֹךְ לְעוֹלָם וָעֶד:
צוּר יִשְׂרָאֵל, קוּמָה בְּעֶזְרַת יִשְׂרָאֵל, וּפְדֵה
כִנְאֻמֶךָ יְהוּדָה וְיִשְׂרָאֵל. גֹּאֲלֵנוּ יהוה
צְבָאוֹת שְׁמוֹ, קְדוֹשׁ יִשְׂרָאֵל.
בָּרוּךְ אַתָּה יהוה, גָּאַל יִשְׂרָאֵל עַמֶּךָ:

Who is like You, Eternal One, among the gods that are worshipped? Who is like You, majestic in holiness, awesome in splendor, doing wonders? The redeemed sang a new song of praise to You on the shores of the sea. Together everyone gave thanks and enthroned You saying: 'Adonai will reign forever and ever.'"
Rock of Israel, rise up and help Israel, redeem us as You promised Judah and Israel. The One whose Name is Adonai Tz'va-ot saves us, the Holy One of Israel. A Source of Blessing are You, Adonai, redeemer of Your people Israel.

Meditation
Our innermost thoughts
are reflected in our body language and action,
even when we think that they are not.
Therefore, speak to yourself only those thoughts
that you want others to see.

[The ARK is OPENED]

If you are comfortable doing so, please rise as we open the ark for the Tefilah (the Prayer) , the Amidah (the time for standing), the central part of our prayers.

אֲדֹנָי שְׂפָתַי תִּפְתָּח וּפִי יַגִּיד תְּהִלָּתֶךָ:

Ado**nai** se**fa**tai tif**tach** u**fi** ya**giyd** tehilatecha.
Eternal God, open my lips, that my mouth may declare Your glory
Oh, God open up my lips, as I begin to pray.
(Psalm 51:17)

If you are more comfortable sitting, please do so at this time or at any time.

The art on this page is called a shviti and traditionally placed on the Eastern wall of a home or where a person chooses to pray at home. We include it here, at the beginning of the Amidah (central prayer) of our service. If you prefer, you are invited to use it as a meditation device for your private prayers.

❦ ❦ ❦ ❦ ❦

We invoke the memories of our spiritual and physical mothers and fathers who made us, the fathers and the mothers who made them and the fathers and the mothers who made them.

We are the product of all of our ancestors as we
stand here in their light before You who made us all.

Each of them sought You and found You in their lives in different ways.
No two of them experienced You the same way. They are the voices behind us.

❦ ❦ ❦ ❦ ❦

GOD OF ALL GENERATIONS   אבות

בָּרוּךְ אַתָּה יהוה אֱלֹהֵינוּ וֵאלֹהֵי אֲבוֹתֵינוּ וְאִמּוֹתֵינוּ, אֱלֹהֵי אַבְרָהָם,
אֱלֹהֵי יִצְחָק, וֵאלֹהֵי יַעֲקֹב, אֱלֹהֵי שָׂרָה, אֱלֹהֵי רִבְקָה, אֱלֹהֵי לֵאָה,
וֵאלֹהֵי רָחֵל. הָאֵל הַגָּדוֹל הַגִּבּוֹר וְהַנּוֹרָא, אֵל עֶלְיוֹן, גּוֹמֵל חֲסָדִים
טוֹבִים, וְקוֹנֵה הַכֹּל, וְזוֹכֵר חַסְדֵי אָבוֹת וְאִמָּהוֹת, וּמֵבִיא גְאֻלָּה לִבְנֵי
בְנֵיהֶם לְמַעַן שְׁמוֹ בְּאַהֲבָה:

♪ **Ba**ruch **ata** Adonai, Ehlo**hei**nu, veilo**hei** avo**tei**nu ve-imo**tei**nu: Elohei
Avra**ham**, Elohei Yitz**chak**, vEilo**hei** Ya-a**kov**. Elo**hei** Sarah, Elohei Rivkah, Elohei
Lei-**ah**, vEilo**hei** Ra**cheil**. Ha-**eil** haga**dol** hagi**bor** vehanora, eil el**yon**, go**meil**
chasa**dim** to**vim** veko**nei** ha**kol**, V'zo**cheir** chas**dei** avot v'ima**hot**, Umeivi g'ula
liv**nei** V'nei**hem**, lema-an sh'**mo**, be-aha**va**:

If you are more comfortable sitting, please do so at this time or at any time.

To Life! High Holy Day Prayer Book

מחזור לחיים

A Source of Blessing are you, Adonai our God and God of our Fathers and our Mothers. God of Abraham, God of Isaac, and God of Jacob, God of Sarah, God of Rebecca, God of Rachel and God of Leah. Great God, powerful and awesome, God of the Highest, who bestows kindness and goodness, master of all, who remembers the good deeds of our fathers and mothers and brings redemption to the children of their children for God's sake with love.

זָכְרֵנוּ לְחַיִּים, מֶלֶךְ חָפֵץ בַּחַיִּים, וְכָתְבֵנוּ בְּסֵפֶר הַחַיִּים, לְמַעַנְךָ אֱלֹהִים חַיִּים. מֶלֶךְ עוֹזֵר וּמוֹשִׁיעַ וּמָגֵן: בָּרוּךְ אַתָּה יהוה, מָגֵן אַבְרָהָם וְעֶזְרַת (וּפוֹקֵד) שָׂרָה:

Zochreinu lechayiym, Melech chafetz bachayiym, vechotveinu beseifer hachayiym, lema-ancha Elohiym chayiym. Melech ozeir umoshi-a umagein: Baruch Ata Adonai, magein Avraham v'ezrat (ufokeid) Sarah.

Remember us for life, O Sovereign who favors life, and write us into the Book of Life, for Your sake, O God of Life, Sovereign who is our Help, our redemption and our protector.
A Blessing are You, Adonai, Shield of Abraham and Helper of (One who remembers) Sarah.

❧❧❧❧❧

Adonai, there was a time for each of us when we felt almost paralyzed with the burdens of life, when everything was overpowering.

We wanted to lie still without moving, feeling almost deadened inside.

And then we turned to You and realized that Your might, Adonai, is everlasting;

Help us use our strength for good and not for evil.

And then we turned to You and realized that You are the support of the falling;

Help us lift up the fallen.

And then we turned to You and realized that You are our hope in death as in life;

Help us keep faith with those who sleep in the dust.

And then we turned to You and realized that Your might, Adonai, is everlasting;

Help us use our strength for good.

Help us to know that it is from you that the radiance comes, that we might rejoice in life itself.

❧❧❧❧❧

If you are more comfortable sitting, please do so at this time or at any time.

G'VUROT / POWER

בורות

אַתָּה גִּבּוֹר לְעוֹלָם אֲדֹנָי מְחַיֵּה הַכֹּל
(מֵתִים) אַתָּה רַב לְהוֹשִׁיעַ:

Atah gibor l'olam Adonai, mechayei hakol (meitiym)
Atah, rav lehoshiy'a.

מוֹרִיד הַטָּל:

Moriyd hatal.   Who brings the dew.

מְכַלְכֵּל חַיִּים בְּחֶסֶד, מְחַיֵּה הַכֹּל (מֵתִים)
בְּרַחֲמִים רַבִּים, סוֹמֵךְ נוֹפְלִים, וְרוֹפֵא
חוֹלִים, וּמַתִּיר אֲסוּרִים, וּמְקַיֵּם אֱמוּנָתוֹ
לִישֵׁנֵי עָפָר, מִי כָמוֹךָ בַּעַל גְּבוּרוֹת וּמִי
דּוֹמֶה לָּךְ, מֶלֶךְ מֵמִית וּמְחַיֶּה וּמַצְמִיחַ יְשׁוּעָה:

Mechalkeil chayim bechesed, mechayei hakol (maytiym) berachamiym rabiym,
someich nofliym verofei choliym umatiyr asuriym, um'kayeim emunato liysheinei
afar, mi chamocha ba-al gevurot umiy domeh lach, melech meymiyt um'chayeh
umatzmiyach yeshu-a.

מִי כָמוֹךָ אַב הָרַחֲמִים, זוֹכֵר יְצוּרָיו לְחַיִּים בְּרַחֲמִים: וְנֶאֱמָן אַתָּה
לְהַחֲיוֹת הַכֹּל (מֵתִים). בָּרוּךְ אַתָּה יהוה, מְחַיֵּה הַכֹּל (מֵתִים):

Mi chamocha Av harachamiym, zocheir yetzurav lechayiym berachamiym.
V'ne-eman Atah lehachayot hakol (maytiym).
Baruch Atah Adonai, mechayei hakol (maytiym).

You are strength forever, Adonai. Giving life to all (the deadened), You are great to
save us. You bring the dew. You support life with mercy, You give life to all (the
deadened) with great compassion. You support the fallen and heal the sick, You
release the captives and establish faith for those who sleep in the dust. Who is like
You, master of strength and who can compare to You, Sovereign of life and death, who
causes salvation to blossom. Who is like You, compassionate parent, who remembers
Your creatures for life with compassion. And You are faithful in giving life to all (the
deadened). A Blessing are You, Adonai, who gives life to all (the deadened).

If you are more comfortable sitting, please do so at this time or at any time.

מחזור לחיים

It is easy to look at the U'netanah Tokef as if it is written by someone very old
Or someone stricken with illness,
Pondering imminent death.

And then I watched a plane
Carrying living human beings
Crash into a building
Full of other living human beings.
And the words struck home:

> *Who will live and who will die*
> *Who in due time and who too suddenly*
> *Who by fire and who by water*
> *Who by sword and who by wild beasts (humans)*
> *Who by starvation and who by dehydration*
> *Who by suffocation and who by hurtling objects.*

And I faced the reality of the gift of life and the recognition that it is a gift
Within a moment of time
What was here is gone.

> *Without warning, we can be thrown*
> *Into explosions, implosions*
> *And horrors beyond belief*
> *Amid the screams of those we love.*

And then I watched a child
Walk among those spending time
With a friend or alone;
He blew himself up in that crowd
And killed those around him
And the words struck home:

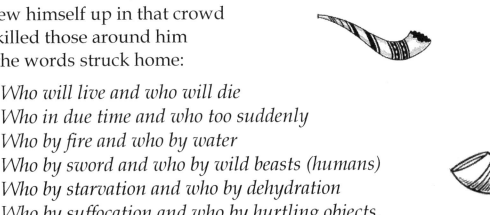

> *Who will live and who will die*
> *Who in due time and who too suddenly*
> *Who by fire and who by water*
> *Who by sword and who by wild beasts (humans)*
> *Who by starvation and who by dehydration*
> *Who by suffocation and who by hurtling objects.*

And I faced the reality of the gift of life and the recognition that it is a gift
Within a moment of time
What was here is gone.

If you are more comfortable sitting, please do so at this time or at any time.

And I watched as Fire
Devoured trees and homes
Destroying all in its path.

And I watched as storms
Pelted the shores,
Drowning those who lingered
In its path too long.

And I watched as cars
Collided with each other
And rolled and crashed.

And I watched as children and adults,
Too thin to eat
Wasted away in lands
Too near and too far away to name.

And the words struck home:
> Who will live and who will die
> Who in due time and who too suddenly

>> *And I heard people asking why God allowed such things*
>> *And I heard people ask where God was, were we abandoned.*

And I realized that God gave us the answers within our Self
If we would only look and do the work.

Perhaps the bitterness of the decree
May be sweetened
By turning into oneself and examining deeds and thoughts

>> *By turning to God for Divine inspiration*
>> *By turning to others and doing God's work*
>> *With our own hands and our own words*

May we find a way this year
To cleanse ourselves of bitterness and anger
To lift up our hearts and minds to Godliness

>> *May we seek righteousness*
>> *May we seek love*
>> *May we seek the Divine in all of us.*

May we hear the Shofar,
May we LIVE LIFE this year.

If you are more comfortable sitting, please do so at this time or at any time.

UNTANEH TOKEF ‏ונתנה תקף‏

‏וּנְתַנֶּה תֹּקֶף קְדֻשַּׁת הַיּוֹם, כִּי הוּא נוֹרָא וְאָיוֹם: וּבוֹ תִנָּשֵׂא מַלְכוּתֶךָ,‏
‏וְיִכּוֹן בְּחֶסֶד כִּסְאֶךָ, וְתֵשֵׁב עָלָיו בֶּאֱמֶת. אֱמֶת כִּי אַתָּה הוּא דַיָּן‏
‏וּמוֹכִיחַ, וְיוֹדֵעַ וָעֵד, וְכוֹתֵב וְחוֹתֵם, וְסוֹפֵר וּמוֹנֶה, וְתִזְכּוֹר כָּל הַנִּשְׁכָּחוֹת:‏
‏וְתִפְתַּח אֶת סֵפֶר הַזִּכְרוֹנוֹת, וּמֵאֵלָיו יִקָּרֵא, וְחוֹתָם יַד כָּל אָדָם בּוֹ.‏

Untaneh **to**kef kedu**shat** ha**yom**, ki hu no**ra** ve-a**yom**: uvo tina**sei** malchu**te**cha, v'yi**kon** be**che**sed kis'echa, vetei**sheiv** a**lav** be-e**met**. **E**met ki **A**ta Hu da**yan** umo**chi**yach, veyo**dei**-a va-**eid**, vecho**teiv** vecho**teim**, veso**feir** umo**neh**, vetiz**kor** kol hanishka**chot**: vetif**tach** et **sei**fer hazichro**not**, umei-ei**lav** yika**rei**, vecho**tam** yad kol **adam** bo.

We acclaim this day's pure sanctity, its awesome power. You record and seal, count and measure, remembering all that we have forgotten. You open the Book of Remembrance and it speaks for itself, for every person has signed it personally.

The great shofar is sounded. A still, small voice is heard. This day even angels are alert, filled with awe and trembling as they declare: "The day of judgment is here!" For even the hosts of heaven are judged. This day all who walk the earth pass before You as a flock of sheep. And like a shepherd who gathers the flock, bringing them under the staff, You bring everything that lives before You for review. You determine life and decree the destiny of every creature.

‏בְּרֹאשׁ הַשָּׁנָה יִכָּתֵבוּן, וּבְיוֹם צוֹם כִּפּוּר יֵחָתֵמוּן,‏

Be**Rosh** HaSha**nah** yikatei**vun**. Uv'**Yom** Tzom Kip**pur** yeichatei**mun**. On Rosh Hashanah it is written And on Yom Kippur it is sealed:

How many will leave this world and how many will be born into it, who will live and who will die, who will live in fullness and who will not, who by fire and who by water, who by sword and who by beast, who by hunger and who by thirst, who by earthquake and who by plague, who by strangling and who by stoning, who will rest and who will wander, who will be at peace and who will be tormented, who will be poor and who will be rich, who will be humbled and who will be exalted.

‏וּתְשׁוּבָה וּתְפִלָּה וּצְדָקָה מַעֲבִירִין אֶת רֹעַ הַגְּזֵרָה.‏

Ut'shu**vah** ut'fi**lah** utzeda**kah** ma-avi**riyn** et **ro**-a hagzei**rah**. And returning to God, prayer and tzedakah avert the harshness of the decree.

If you are more comfortable sitting, please do so at this time or at any time.

Nekadesh/Kedushah/Holiness   נקדש\קדושה

נְקַדֵּשׁ אֶת שִׁמְךָ בָּעוֹלָם, כְּשֵׁם שֶׁמַּקְדִּישִׁים אוֹתוֹ בִּשְׁמֵי מָרוֹם,

כַּכָּתוּב עַל יַד נְבִיאֶךָ, וְקָרָא זֶה אֶל זֶה וְאָמַר:

Nekadeish et shim**cha** ba-olam k'**sheim** shemakdiy**shiym** oto bish'**mei** ma**rom**,
ka**katuv** al yad n'vi-**echa** v'**kara** zeh el zeh v'**amar**:

We sanctify Your name for all time and space, just as Your Holy Name was sanctified in the highest places, as it was written by the hand of Your prophets, and they [the angels] called out to each other:

קָדוֹשׁ קָדוֹשׁ קָדוֹשׁ יהוה צְבָאוֹת, מְלֹא כָל הָאָרֶץ כְּבוֹדוֹ.

Ka**dosh** ka**dosh** ka**dosh** Ado**nai** Tz'va-ot, me**lo** chol ha-**aretz** kevo**do**.

Holy, Holy, Holy are You, Adonai Tz'va-ot, all the earth is filled with Your glory.

אַדִּיר אַדִּירֵנוּ, יהוה אֲדֹנֵינוּ, מָה אַדִּיר שִׁמְךָ בְּכָל הָאָרֶץ.

A**diyr** adiy**reinu**, Ado**nai** Ado**neinu**, mah a**diyr** shim**cha** be**chol** ha-aretz.

Strength of our strength, connectivity of our connectivity, how mighty is Your Name in all the earth.

  בָּרוּךְ כְּבוֹד יהוה, מִמְּקוֹמוֹ.

Baruch ke**vod** Ado**nai** mimko**mo**.

A source of Blessing is Adonai's glory, radiating from the Source.

אֶחָד הוּא אֱלֹהֵינוּ, הוּא אָבִינוּ, הוּא מַלְכֵּנוּ, הוּא מוֹשִׁיעֵנוּ,

וְהוּא יַשְׁמִיעֵנוּ בְּרַחֲמָיו שֵׁנִית לְעֵינֵי כָּל חָי:

Hu Elo**heinu**, Hu A**vinu**, Hu Mal**keinu**, Hu Moshi-**einu**, veHu Yashmi-**einu** beracha**mav**
shei**niyt** l'**einei** kol chai.

One is our God, God is our parent, God is our Sovereign, God is our salvation. And God will declare again with compassion for the eyes of all that live:

אֲנִי יהוה אֱלֹהֵיכֶם!

Ani Ado**nai** Elohei**chem**

I am Adonai your God.

יִמְלֹךְ יהוה לְעוֹלָם, אֱלֹהַיִךְ צִיּוֹן לְדֹר וָדֹר, הַלְלוּיָהּ.

Yim**loch** Ado**nai** l'**olam**, eloha**yich** tzi**yon** le**dor** va**dor**. Hallelu-**Yahh**.

Adonai will reign forever, Your God, Tzion, from generation to generation. Praise Yahh (Adonai).

לְדוֹר וָדוֹר נַגִּיד גָּדְלֶךָ וּלְנֵצַח נְצָחִים קְדֻשָּׁתְךָ נַקְדִּישׁ, וְשִׁבְחֲךָ

אֱלֹהֵינוּ מִפִּינוּ לֹא יָמוּשׁ לְעוֹלָם וָעֶד, כִּי אֵל מֶלֶךְ גָּדוֹל וְקָדוֹשׁ אָתָּה.

L'**dor** va**dor** na**giyd** god**lecha** ul'**neitzach** n'tza**chiym** kedushat**cha** nak**diysh**.
V'shivcha**cha** Elo**heinu** mi**pinu** lo ya**mush** l'olam va-ed. Ki Eil **Me**lech ga**dol**
veka**dosh A**tah.

We sing and praise the Holy One.

For the children and their children, (We) bless the Light.

If you are more comfortable sitting, please do so at this time or at any time.

From generation to generation, we will tell of Your greatness and for all time we will sanctify Your holiness. O God, Your praise will never vanish from our lips, for you are a great and Holy Divine Sovereign.

❄❄❄❄❄

אַתָּה קָדוֹשׁ וְשִׁמְךָ קָדוֹשׁ וּקְדוֹשִׁים בְּכָל יוֹם יְהַלְלוּךָ, סֶּלָה.

Ata ka**dosh** veshim**cha** ka**dosh** ukdo**shiym** be**chol** yom yehale**lu**cha, **Se**la.

You are holiness and Your Name is Holy, we praise your holiness every day, Selah.

❄❄❄❄❄

U'VECHEIN

וּבְכֵן

U'vechein, Make all creatures awestruck at Your greatness. Help all life align their desires with Yours, with full harmony of heart, sharing in Your glory. Bring us hope in Your promise, joy in our land, delight in Your city, Jerusalem.

Then Your power will be the only one we know, and holiness will rule from the City of Peace, Your Shechina's dwelling. So we sing:

יִמְלֹךְ יהוה לְעוֹלָם, אֱלֹהַיִךְ צִיּוֹן לְדֹר וָדֹר: הַלְלוּיָהּ.

All: *Yimloch Adonai l'olam, Elohayich Tzion, Ledor vador, HalleluYahh!*

Holy Awesome One! There is none like You!

You have chosen us to serve You by loving us and giving us Your guidance through Torah and mitzvot, through which we link ourselves to You.

R. Marcia Prager, adapted

❄❄❄❄❄

בָּרוּךְ אַתָּה יהוה, הַמֶּלֶךְ הַקָּדוֹשׁ.

Baruch **A**ta, Ado**nai** ha-**Me**lech ha**Ka**dosh.

A Blessing are You, Adonai, the Holy Sovereign.

We are seated.

❄❄❄❄❄

אֱלֹהֵינוּ וֵאלֹהֵי אֲבוֹתֵינוּ וְאִמּוֹתֵינוּ, תָּבֹא לְפָנֶיךָ תְּפִלָּתֵנוּ, וְאַל תִּתְעַלַּם מִתְּחִנָּתֵנוּ, שֶׁאֵין אָנוּ עַזֵּי פָנִים וּקְשֵׁי עֹרֶף לוֹמַר לְפָנֶיךָ, יהוה אֱלֹהֵינוּ וֵאלֹהֵי אֲבוֹתֵינוּ וְאִמּוֹתֵינוּ, צַדִּיקִים אֲנַחְנוּ וְלֹא חָטָאנוּ, אֲבָל אֲנַחְנוּ וַאֲבוֹתֵינוּ וְאִמּוֹתֵינוּ חָטָאנוּ.

Elo**hei**nu velo**hei** avo**tei**nu veimo**tei**nu, ta**vo** lefa**ne**cha tefila**tei**nu v'**al** tit'**al**am mitchina**tei**nu, she-**ein anu azei** fa**niym** uk**shei o**ref, lo**mar** lefa**ne**cha Ado**nai** Elo**hei**nu veilo**hei** avo**tei**nu veimo**tei**nu, tzadi**kiym anach**nu ve**lo** cha**ta**nu, a**val anach**nu va-avo**tei**nu veimo**tei**nu cha**ta**nu.

Our God and the God of our fathers and mothers, we bring our prayers before You, so that You not disregard them, for we are not so arrogant or stiff necked as to say before You, our God and the God of our fathers and mothers, that we are pious and have not sinned, for we and our fathers and mothers have sinned.

❦❦❦❦❦

❦❦❦❦❦ ❦❦❦❦❦

Meditation

Rabbi Johanan said it in the name of Rabbi Simeon bar Yochai: It is better for a person to cast him or herself into a fiery furnace rather than put another person to shame in public. (B. Talmud, Brachot)

❦❦❦❦❦ ❦❦❦❦❦

כִּי אָנוּ עַמֶּךָ, וְאַתָּה מַלְכֵּנוּ;
Ki **anu** am**e**cha, v'**A**ta Mal**kei**nu

אָנוּ בָנֶיךָ, וְאַתָּה אָבִינוּ.
Anu van**e**cha, v'**A**ta **A**vinu

אָנוּ נַחֲלָתֶךָ, וְאַתָּה גוֹרָלֵנוּ;
Anu nachala**te**cha, v'**A**ta gora**lei**nu

אָנוּ צֹאנֶךָ, וְאַתָּה רוֹעֵנוּ.
Anu tzon**e**cha, v'**A**ta ro-**ei**nu

אָנוּ כַרְמֶךָ, וְאַתָּה נוֹטְרֵנוּ;
Anu char**me**cha, v'**A**ta not**rei**nu

אָנוּ רַעְיָתֶךָ, וְאַתָּה דוֹדֵנוּ;
Anu raya**te**cha, v'**A**ta do**dei**nu.

For we are Your people and You are our Sovereign,
We are Your children and You are our Parent,
We are Your legacy and You are our Destiny,
We are Your sheep and You are our Shepherd,
We are Your vineyard and You are our Guardian,
We are Your partner and You are our Beloved.

❦❦❦❦❦

If Yom Kippur falls on Shabbat, please add { }:

בָּרוּךְ אַתָּה יהוה, מְקַדֵּשׁ {הַשַּׁבָּת וְ} יִשְׂרָאֵל וְיוֹם הַכִּפּוּרִים:

Baruch **A**ta Ado**nai**, meka**deish** {ha**Sha**bat v'}Yisra-**eil** ve**yom** hakipu**riym**.

A Blessing are You, Adonai, who makes holy {the Shabbat and} Israel and this day of approaching.

❦❦❦❦❦

בָּרוּךְ אַתָּה יהוה, הַמַּחֲזִיר שְׁכִינָתוֹ לְצִיּוֹן.

Baruch **A**ta Ado**nai**, hamacha**zir** shechina**to** l'tzi**yon**.

A Source of Blessing are You, Adonai, who returns Shechina to Tzion.

❦❦❦❦❦❦

In some special way every person completes the universe.
> *If I do not play my part,*
> *I injure the pattern of all existence.*

The same stream of life
that runs through my veins night and day
runs through the world and dances in rhythmic measures.
> *It is the same life that shoots in joy*
> *through the dust of the earth in numberless blades of grass*
> *and breaks into tumultuous waves of leaves and flowers.*

Thank You for the gift of Your Love and of Hope,
Thank You for Your Loving and Forgiving Presence in our lives.

❦❦❦❦❦❦

בָּרוּךְ אַתָּה יהוה, הַטּוֹב שִׁמְךָ וּלְךָ נָאֶה לְהוֹדוֹת.

Baruch **A**ta Ado**nai**, ha**tov** shim**cha** ule**cha** na-**eh** leho**dot**.

A Source of Blessing are You, Adonai, whose Essence is goodness and who is worthy of our thanks.

❦❦❦❦❦

Adonai, it is not easy to look inside and see what I am hiding deep inside.
And yet, when I think I can hide from You
I am only lying to myself, for You see.

> Your love and blessing keep me safe, even from myself.
> Your love and blessing allow me to look inside
> and own my responsibilities,
> Even when I would still rather think
> that others are the cause of all of my troubles.
>> *When I can, in fact, own my own responsibilities*
> *And be accountable for my actions to myself, to You and to others,*
> *Then I open myself to Your blessings and Your abundance.*

❦❦❦❦❦

♪ יְבָרֶכְךָ יהוה וְיִשְׁמְרֶךָ.   כֵּן יְהִי רָצוֹן

Y'varechecha Adonai v'yishmerecha.   Kein yehi ratzon.
May Adonai bless you and protect you.

יָאֵר יהוה פָּנָיו אֵלֶיךָ וִיחֻנֶּךָּ.   כֵּן יְהִי רָצוֹן

Ya-eir Adonai panav eilecha vichuneka.   Kein yehi ratzon.
May Adonai shine God's countenance on you with wisdom and grace.

יִשָּׂא יהוה פָּנָיו אֵלֶיךָ וְיָשֵׂם לְךָ שָׁלוֹם.   כֵּן יְהִי רָצוֹן

Yisa Adonai panav eilecha v'yaseim lecha shalom.   Kein yehi ratzon.
May Adonai lift God's countenance onto you and grant you shalom, peace and wholeness.

We offer to You again, the prayer for peace:
"Peace to those near and to those far off."
For the Prophets teach: If others are in turmoil and
disharmony rules their lives, there can be no peace for us.
When the noise of our lives drowns out the music for which we yearn,
others likewise can find no peace.

שָׁלוֹם

              Peace for all Israel. Peace for all humankind.

♪ בָּרוּךְ אַתָּה יהוה, עוֹשֶׂה הַשָּׁלוֹם.

Baruch Ata Adonai, oseh hashalom.
Blessings are You, Adonai, who makes peace.

 WE PRAY SILENTLY

עֹשֶׂה שָׁלוֹם בִּמְרוֹמָיו הוּא יַעֲשֶׂה שָׁלוֹם עָלֵינוּ וְעַל כָּל יִשְׂרָאֵל,
♪ (וְעַל כָּל יוֹשְׁבֵי תֵבֵל,) וְאִמְרוּ אָמֵן:

Oseh shalom bimromav, hu ya-aseh shalom aleinu, v'al kol Yisra-eil, (v'al kol
yoshvei teyveil,) v'imru: amein.
May the One who makes peace in the high places, make peace for us and for Israel and
all the world, and let us say, Amen.

♪ שְׁמַע קוֹלֵנוּ, יהוה אֱלֹהֵינוּ, חוּס וְרַחֵם עָלֵינוּ, וְקַבֵּל בְּרַחֲמִים
♪ וּבְרָצוֹן אֶת תְּפִלָּתֵנוּ. כִּי אֵל שׁוֹמֵעַ תְּפִלּוֹת וְתַחֲנוּנִים אָתָּה.

Sh'ma koleinu, Adonai Eloheinu, chus v'racheim aleinu, v'kabeil berachamiym
uvratzon et tefilateinu. Ki Eil shomei-a tefilot v'tachanuniym Ata.
Hear our voice, Adonai our God. Have pity and mercy on us and receive our prayers with compassion and favor. For You
are a God who listens to prayers and supplications.

אָשַׁמְנוּ, בָּגַדְנוּ, גָּזַלְנוּ, דִּבַּרְנוּ דֹפִי.

Ashamnu, bagadnu, gazalnu, dibarnu dofi.

הֶעֱוִינוּ, וְהִרְשַׁעְנוּ, זַדְנוּ, חָמַסְנוּ, טָפַלְנוּ שֶׁקֶר.

He-evinu, vehirsha'nu, zadnu, chamasnu, tafalnu sheker

יָעַצְנוּ רָע, כִּזַּבְנוּ, לַצְנוּ, מָרַדְנוּ, נִאַצְנוּ,

Ya-atznu ra, kizavnu, latznu, maradnu, ni-atznu

סָרַרְנוּ, עָוִינוּ, פָּשַׁעְנוּ, צָרַרְנוּ, קִשִּׁינוּ עֹרֶף.

Sararnu, avinu, pasha-nu, tzararnu, kishinu oref

רָשַׁעְנוּ, שִׁחַתְנוּ, תִּעַבְנוּ, תָּעִינוּ, תִּעְתָּעְנוּ.

Rasha-nu, shichatnu, ti-avnu, ta-iynu, ti'-ta'-nu.

We all have committed offenses; together we confess these human sins:

We've been **A**rrogant, We've been **B**igoted,
    We've been **C**ynical; We've been **D**eceitful;

We've been **E**gotistical, We've been **F**latterers;
    We've been **G**reedy, We've been **H**aughty,

We've been **I**njust; We've been **J**ealous.
    We've **K**ept grudges, We've been **L**ustful,

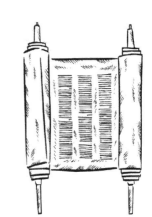

We've been **M**alicious; We've been **N**arrow-minded.
    We've been **O**bstinate, We've been **P**ossessive,

We've been **Q**uarrelsome, We've been **R**ancorous;
    We've been **S**elfish. We've been **V**iolent,

We've been **W**eak-willed, We've been **X**enophobic.
    We've **Y**ielded to temptation; We've shown **Z**eal for bad causes.

Now may it be Your will, Adonai, God of all the generations, to pardon all our sins, to forgive all our wrong-doings, and to blot out all our transgressions:

AL CHEIT   על חטא

On Yom Kippur, we take collective responsibility for our lives and the life of the community in which we live. We are all responsible to each other and we, as Jews, a never allowed to sit back and let "someone else" carry the burden alone. Judaism is not a "consumer religion."

Although we realize that we did not create the world we were born into, we nevertheless have a responsibility for what it is like as long as we are part of it. And although we are heavily conditioned in our childhood to be a certain way, we also have a responsibility to transcend that conditioning and take charge of our own lives, to remake community, and to create the conditions in which our freedom can be actualized.

And to the extent that we have failed to do all that we could in the past year, we ask ourselves for COLLECTIVE forgiveness.

עַל חֵטְא שֶׁחָטָאנוּ לְפָנֶיךָ בְּאֹנֶס וּבְרָצוֹן,
וְעַל חֵטְא שֶׁחָטָאנוּ לְפָנֶיךָ בְּאִמּוּץ הַלֵּב.

Al cheit shechatanu lefanecha b'ones uvratzon;
V'al cheit shechatanu lefanecha b'imutz haleiv.
For the sin we have sinned before You unwillingly or willingly;
For the sin we have sinned before You through heart or mind.

V'al cheit shechatanu lefanecha ...   ... וְעַל חֵטְא שֶׁחָטָאנוּ לְפָנֶיךָ

For the sins we have committed before You and before us
    by being so tired of hearing about suffering
    that finally we closed our ears
And For the sins we have committed before You and before us
    by crying so much to others about suffering
    that finally they closed their ears.

V'al cheit shechatanu lefanecha ...   ... וְעַל חֵטְא שֶׁחָטָאנוּ לְפָנֶיךָ

For the sins we have committed before You and before us
    by blaming ourselves for those things which were beyond our control
And For the sins we have committed before You and before us
    by not taking action when it was simple
    and/or within our control and we knew it would have an impact.

וְעַל כֻּלָּם, אֱלוֹהַ סְלִיחוֹת, סְלַח לָנוּ, מְחַל לָנוּ, כַּפֶּר-לָנוּ.

V'al kulam Eloha selichot. Selach lanu, mechal lanu, kaper lanu.
For all these we ask the One and each other for forgiveness.

וְעַל חֵטְא שֶׁחָטָאנוּ לְפָנֶיךָ ...

V'**al** cheit shechatanu lefanecha ...

For the sins we have committed before You and before us
    by thinking no one would really care, that we were alone
    and that there was no point in reaching out to others
And For the sins we have committed before You and before us
    by thinking that the temporary powerlessness
    was permanent and would never change.

... וְעַל חֵטְא שֶׁחָטָאנוּ לְפָנֶיךָ

V'**al** cheit shecha**ta**nu lefa**ne**cha ...

For the sins we have committed before You and before us
    by being judgmental of others and ourselves
And For the sins we have committed before You and before us
    by not having compassion for others
    when they are reacting out of fear and anger.

... וְעַל חֵטְא שֶׁחָטָאנוּ לְפָנֶיךָ

V'**al** cheit shecha**ta**nu lefanecha ...

For the sins we have committed before You and before us
    by not forgiving our parents for what they did to us when we were children
And For the sins we have committed before You and before us
    by not forgiving ourselves for what we have done to our children.

... וְעַל חֵטְא שֶׁחָטָאנוּ לְפָנֶיךָ

V'**al** cheit shecha**ta**nu lefa**ne**cha ...

For the sins we have committed before You and before us
    by not forgiving ourselves
    for the traits and habits and dispositions we inherited
And For the sins we have committed before You and before us
    by not working to improve those traits and habits and dispositions of ours
    that harm others and ourselves.

... וְעַל חֵטְא שֶׁחָטָאנוּ לְפָנֶיךָ

V'**al** cheit shecha**ta**nu lefa**ne**cha ...

For the sins we have committed before You and before us
    by not seeing the spark of the Divine in each person we encounter
And For the sins we have committed before You and before us
    by not being in touch with our own Divinity.

וְעַל כֻּלָּם, אֱלוֹהַּ סְלִיחוֹת, סְלַח לָנוּ, מְחַל לָנוּ, כַּפֶּר-לָנוּ.

V'**al** ku**lam** Elo**ha** seli**chot**. Se**lach la**nu, me**chal la**nu, ka**per la**nu.

For all these we ask the One and each other for forgiveness.

✤✤✤✤✤

[The ARK is OPENED]
If you are comfortable doing so, please rise as we open the ark for Avinu Malkeinu

אָבִינוּ מַלְכֵּנוּ! שְׁמַע קוֹלֵנוּ.

Avinu Malkeinu! Sh'ma koleinu.
Avinu Malkeynu! Hear our plea.

אָבִינוּ מַלְכֵּנוּ! חָטָאנוּ לְפָנֶיךָ.

Avinu Malkeinu! Chatanu lefanecha.
Avinu Malkeynu! We have sinned.

אָבִינוּ מַלְכֵּנוּ! חֲמוֹל עָלֵינוּ וְעַל עוֹלָלֵנוּ וְטַפֵּנוּ.

Avinu Malkeinu! Chamol aleinu v'al olaleinu vetapeinu.
Avinu Malkeynu! Have mercy on us and on our children.

אָבִינוּ מַלְכֵּנוּ! כַּלֵּה דֶּבֶר וְחֶרֶב וְרָעָב מֵעָלֵינוּ.

Avinu Malkeinu! Kalei dever v'cherev v'ra'av mey-aleinu.
Avinu Malkeynu! Help us diminish pestilence, war and famine.

אָבִינוּ מַלְכֵּנוּ! כַּלֵּה כָּל צַר וּמַשְׂטִין מֵעָלֵינוּ.

Avinu Malkeinu! Kalei kol tzar umistiyn mei-aleinu.
Avinu Malkeynu! Help us diminish hate and oppresion.

אָבִינוּ מַלְכֵּנוּ! כָּתְבֵנוּ בְּסֵפֶר חַיִּים טוֹבִים.

Avinu Malkeinu! Kotveinu beseifer chayiym toviym.
Avinu Malkeynu! Enter us into the Book of Life

אָבִינוּ מַלְכֵּנוּ! חַדֵּשׁ עָלֵינוּ שָׁנָה טוֹבָה.

Avinu Malkeinu! Chadeish aleinu shanah tovah.
Avinu Malkeynu! Renew our faith in the future that we may make the coming year truly a shanah tovah, a year of goodness.

אָבִינוּ מַלְכֵּנוּ! חָנֵּנוּ וַעֲנֵנוּ, כִּי אֵין בָּנוּ מַעֲשִׂים, עֲשֵׂה עִמָּנוּ צְדָקָה וָחֶסֶד וְהוֹשִׁיעֵנוּ.

Avinu Malkeinu! Chaneinu va'aneinu, ki ein banu ma-asiym, asei imanu tzedakah vachesed vehoshi-einu.
Avinu Malkeynu! Please be gracious and answer us, for we have not earned it; please help us to do right through Tzedakah and be a conduit for Your mercy that we might become worthy.

The ARK is CLOSED and we are seated.

Full Kaddish

יִתְגַּדַּל וְיִתְקַדַּשׁ שְׁמֵהּ רַבָּא. בְּעָלְמָא דִּי בְרָא כִרְעוּתֵיהּ, וְיַמְלִיךְ מַלְכוּתֵיהּ בְּחַיֵּיכוֹן וּבְיוֹמֵיכוֹן וּבְחַיֵּי דְכָל בֵּית יִשְׂרָאֵל. בַּעֲגָלָא וּבִזְמַן קָרִיב וְאִמְרוּ אָמֵן:

Yitgadal v'yitkadash shimei raba b'alma di v'ra chirutei, v'yamlich malchutei b'chayeichon uv'yomeichon uv'chayei d'chol beit Yisra-eil, ba-agala, ba-agala, uvizman kariv, v'im'ru: Amein.

יְהֵא שְׁמֵהּ רַבָּא מְבָרַךְ לְעָלַם וּלְעָלְמֵי עָלְמַיָּא:

Yehei sh'mei raba m'varach l'alam ul'almei almaya.

יִתְבָּרַךְ וְיִשְׁתַּבַּח וְיִתְפָּאַר וְיִתְרוֹמַם וְיִתְנַשֵּׂא וְיִתְהַדָּר וְיִתְעַלֶּה וְיִתְהַלָּל שְׁמֵהּ דְּקֻדְשָׁא בְּרִיךְ הוּא לְעֵלָּא לְעֵלָּא מִכָּל בִּרְכָתָא וְשִׁירָתָא תֻּשְׁבְּחָתָא וְנֶחֱמָתָא, דַּאֲמִירָן בְּעָלְמָא, וְאִמְרוּ אָמֵן:

Yitbarach, v'yishtabach, v'yitpa-ar, v'yitromam, v'yitnasei, v'yit-hadar, v'yit-aleh, v'yit-halal sh'mei d'kudsha, brich hu. L'eila l'eila mikol birchata v'shirata, tushb'chata v'nechemata da-amiran b'alma, v'im'ru: Amein.

תִּתְקַבֵּל צְלוֹתְהוֹן וּבָעוּתְהוֹן דְּכָל בֵּית יִשְׂרָאֵל קֳדָם אֲבוּהוֹן דִּי בִשְׁמַיָּא וְאִמְרוּ אָמֵן:

Titkabeil tzelot'hon uva-ut'hon dechol Beit Yisra-eil kadam avuhon di vishmaya, v'imru: amein.

יְהֵא שְׁלָמָא רַבָּא מִן שְׁמַיָּא, וְחַיִּים עָלֵינוּ וְעַל כָּל יִשְׂרָאֵל וְאִמְרוּ אָמֵן.

Y'hei sh'lama raba min sh'maya, v'chayim aleinu v'al kol Yisra-eil, v'imru: amein.

עֹשֶׂה שָׁלוֹם בִּמְרוֹמָיו הוּא יַעֲשֶׂה שָׁלוֹם עָלֵינוּ וְעַל כָּל יִשְׂרָאֵל, (וְעַל כָּל יוֹשְׁבֵי תֵבֵל,) וְאִמְרוּ אָמֵן:

Oseh shalom bimromav, hu ya-aseh shalom aleinu, v'al kol Yisra-eil, (v'al kol yoshvei teyveil,) v'imru: amein.

God's glory is to be extolled, God's great Name to be hallowed in the world whose creation God willed. And may God's reign be in our day, during our life, and the life of all Israel, let us say: Amen.
Let God's great Name be praised forever and ever.
Let the Name of the Holy One, the Blessing One, be glorified, exalted, and honored, though God is beyond all the praises, songs, and adorations that we can utter, and let us say: Amen.
Receive at once the prayers and pleas of all of the House of Israel, our Parent in Heaven, and let us say: Amen.
May there be abundant peace from heaven and life for us and all Israel, and let us say: Amen.
May the One who makes peace in the high places make peace for us and for all of Israel (and all the world), and let us say: Amen.

TORAH SERVICE

If you are comfortable doing so, please rise as we open the ark for the Torah

כִּי מִצִּיּוֹן תֵּצֵא תוֹרָה , וּדְבַר יהוה מִירוּשָׁלָיִם:

בָּרוּךְ שֶׁנָתַן תּוֹרָה לְעַמּוֹ יִשְׂרָאֵל בִּקְדֻשָׁתוֹ:

Ki mi-tzi**yon** tei**tzei** to**rah**, ud'var Ado**nai** mirusha**la**yim.
Ba**ruch** she-na**tan** to**rah** l'**amo** Yisra-**eil** bik'dusha**to**.

For from Tzion, Torah goes forth and the word of Adonai from Jerusalem.
A Source of Blessing is the One who gave Torah to God's people Israel in holiness.

יהוה, יהוה, אֵל רַחוּם וְחַנּוּן, אֶרֶךְ אַפַּיִם, וְרַב חֶסֶד

וֶאֱמֶת: נֹצֵר חֶסֶד לָאֲלָפִים, נֹשֵׂא עָוֹן וָפֶשַׁע וְחַטָּאָה, וְנַקֵּה:

Ado**nai** Ado**nai** eil ra**chum** vecha**nun**, **e**rech a**pa**yim ve**rav che**sed ve-e**met**,
no**tzeir che**sed la-ala**fiym**, no**sei** a**von** va**fe**sha vechata-**ah** vena**kei**.

Adonai, Adonai, God of compassion and grace, slow to anger and abounding with mercy and truth.
You grant mercy to the thousands, lifting shame and inequity and sin; You are cleansing.

(The Torah is removed from the Ark.)

CALL AND RESPONSE (leader, then congregation):

שְׁמַע יִשְׂרָאֵל, יהוה אֱלֹהֵינוּ, יהוה אֶחָד.

Shema Yisra-**eil**, Ado**nai** Elo**heinu**, Ado**nai** e**chad**!

Hear, O Israel, Adonai is our God, Adonai is One.

אֶחָד אֱלֹהֵינוּ, גָּדוֹל אֲדוֹנֵנוּ, קָדוֹשׁ וְנוֹרָא שְׁמוֹ.

Echad Elo**heinu** ga**dol** ado**neinu** ka**dosh** veno**rah** Sh'**mo**.

Our God is One; Adonai is great; holy and awesome is God's Name.

Together:

גַּדְּלוּ לַיהוה אִתִּי, וּנְרוֹמְמָה שְׁמוֹ יַחְדָּו.

Ga**dlu** l'Ado**nai** iti, un'rom'**mah** sh'**mo** yach'**dav**.

Acknowledge Adonai's greatness with me, and let us exalt God's Name together.

לְךָ יהוה הַגְּדֻלָּה וְהַגְּבוּרָה וְהַתִּפְאֶרֶת וְהַנֵּצַח וְהַהוֹד, כִּי כֹל בַּשָּׁמַיִם וּבָאָרֶץ: לְךָ יהוה הַמַּמְלָכָה וְהַמִּתְנַשֵּׂא לְכֹל לְרֹאשׁ.

Lecha Adonai hagedula vehagevura vehatif-eret vehaneitzach vehahod, ki chol bashamayim uva-aretz: **Lecha Adonai** hamamlacha vehamitnasei lechol lerosh.

Yours, Adonai, is the greatness, the power, the glory, the victory, and the majesty; for all that is in heaven and earth is Yours. Yours is the kingdom, Adonai, You are supreme over all.

עַל שְׁלֹשָׁה דְבָרִים הָעוֹלָם עוֹמֵד, עַל הַתּוֹרָה וְעַל הָעֲבוֹדָה וְעַל גְּמִילוּת חֲסָדִים

Al shlosha devariym, ha-olam omeid.
Al haTorah v'al ha-avodah, v'al gemilut chasadiym.

The world depends on three things: on Torah, on worship and on loving deeds.

Once the Torah is resting on the table, we are seated.

TORAH BLESSING (Before Reading)

בָּרְכוּ אֶת יהוה הַמְּבוֹרָךְ.
Barchu et A**do**nai hamevo**rach**.
We praise Adonai, the Source of Blessing, Who blesses.

בָּרוּךְ יהוה הַמְּבֹרָךְ לְעוֹלָם וָעֶד:
Baruch A**do**nai hamevo**rach** l'**olam** va-**ed**.
Praised be Adonai, the Source of Blessing, now and forever.

בָּרוּךְ אַתָּה יהוה אֱלֹהֵינוּ מֶלֶךְ הָעוֹלָם, אֲשֶׁר בָּחַר בָּנוּ עִם (מִ-)כָּל הָעַמִים וְנָתַן לָנוּ אֶת תּוֹרָתוֹ: בָּרוּךְ אַתָּה יהוה, נוֹתֵן הַתּוֹרָה.

Baruch Ata Adonai, E**lo**heinu **Melech** ha-olam asher bachar banu im (mi)**kol** ha-**amiym**, Vena**tan lanu** et Tora**to**.
Baruch Ata Adonai, no**tein** ha**Torah**.

Blessed is Adonai, our God, Sovereign of the universe, who has chosen us with (from) all peoples and has given us Torah. A Source of Blessing is Adonai, Giver of the Torah.

Torah Reading - Numbers

כט וְהָיְתָה לָכֶם לְחֻקַּת עוֹלָם בַּחֹדֶשׁ הַשְּׁבִיעִי בֶּעָשׂוֹר לַחֹדֶשׁ תְּעַנּוּ אֶת־נַפְשֹׁתֵיכֶם וְכָל־מְלָאכָה לֹא תַעֲשׂוּ הָאֶזְרָח וְהַגֵּר הַגָּר בְּתוֹכְכֶם:

Vehaitah lachem lechukat olam bachodesh hashvi-i be-asor lachodesh t'anu et nafshoteichem vechol melachah lo ta-asu ha-ezrach vehageir hagar betochachem.

16:29 And this will be an eternal statute (*chuk*) for you. In the 7th month, on the 10th day, answer with your soul and do not do any work - neither the native born nor the ones who dwell in your midst.

ל כִּי־בַיּוֹם הַזֶּה יְכַפֵּר עֲלֵיכֶם לְטַהֵר אֶתְכֶם מִכֹּל חַטֹּאתֵיכֶם לִפְנֵי יְהוָה תִּטְהָרוּ:

Ki vayom hazeh yechapeir aleichem letaheir etchem mikol chatoteichem lifnei Adonai titharu.

16:30 For on this day you will atone for yourselves, to purify yourselves from all of your sinning; before Adonai, you will purify yourselves.

לא שַׁבַּת שַׁבָּתוֹן הִיא לָכֶם וְעִנִּיתֶם אֶת־נַפְשֹׁתֵיכֶם חֻקַּת עוֹלָם:

Shabat Shabaton hi lachem v'iniytem et nafshoteichem chukat olam.

16:31 It is a "Shabbat of Shabbat" to you, and you will answer with your soul. This is a *chuk* forever.

לב וְכִפֶּר הַכֹּהֵן אֲשֶׁר־יִמְשַׁח אֹתוֹ וַאֲשֶׁר יְמַלֵּא אֶת־יָדוֹ לְכַהֵן תַּחַת אָבִיו וְלָבַשׁ אֶת־בִּגְדֵי הַבָּד בִּגְדֵי הַקֹּדֶשׁ:

Vechiper hakohein asher yimshach oto va-asher yemalei et yado lechahein tachat aviv velavash et bigdei habad bigdei hakodesh.

16:32 And the Koheyn whom you anointed and who fills his hands with ministering in place of his father will do the atoning and wear the linen vestments, the sacred vestments.

לג וְכִפֶּר אֶת־מִקְדַּשׁ הַקֹּדֶשׁ וְאֶת־אֹהֶל מוֹעֵד וְאֶת־הַמִּזְבֵּחַ יְכַפֵּר וְעַל הַכֹּהֲנִים וְעַל־כָּל־עַם הַקָּהָל יְכַפֵּר:

Vechiper et mikdash hakodesh v'et Ohel Mo-eid v'et hamizbei-ach yechapeir v'al hakohaniym v'al kol am hakahal yechapeir.

16:33 And he will atone and sanctify the sanctuary and atone the Tent of Seasons and the altar. And over the Koheyn and over all of the people, the community will atone.

לד וְהָיְתָה־זֹּאת לָכֶם לְחֻקַּת עוֹלָם לְכַפֵּר עַל־בְּנֵי יִשְׂרָאֵל מִכָּל־חַטֹּאתָם אַחַת בַּשָּׁנָה וַיַּעַשׂ כַּאֲשֶׁר צִוָּה יְהוָה אֶת־מֹשֶׁה:

Vehaitah zot lachem lechukat olam lechapeir al benei Yisra-eil mikol chatotam achat bashanah vaya-as ka-asher tzivah Adonai et Moshe.

16:34 And this will be a *chuk* for you, to atone over the Children of Israel from all of their sinning once each year. And they did as Adonai had instructed Moshe.

❀❀❀❀❀

TORAH BLESSING (After Reading)

בָּרוּךְ אַתָּה יהוה אֱלֹהֵינוּ מֶלֶךְ הָעוֹלָם, אֲשֶׁר נָתַן לָנוּ תּוֹרַת
אֱמֶת, וְחַיֵּי עוֹלָם נָטַע בְּתוֹכֵנוּ. בָּרוּךְ אַתָּה יהוה, נוֹתֵן הַתּוֹרָה.

Baruch Ata Adonai Eloheinu Melech ha-olam, asher natan lanu torat emet,
vechayei olam nata betocheinu. Baruch Ata Adonai notein haTorah.

A Source of Blessing is Adonai, our God, Sovereign of the universe, who has given us a Torah of truth, implanting it within us. A Source of Blessing is Adonai, Giver of the Torah.

❀❀❀❀❀

Prayer for healing

מִי שֶׁבֵּרַךְ אֲבוֹתֵינוּ מְקוֹר הַבְּרָכָה לְאִמּוֹתֵינוּ

Mi shebeirach avoteinu mekor habracha le-imoteinu.
May the source of strength who blessed the ones before us
Help us find the courage to make our lives a blessing. And let us say -- Amen.

מִי שֶׁבֵּרַךְ אִמּוֹתֵינוּ מְקוֹר הַבְּרָכָה לַאֲבוֹתֵינוּ

Mi shebeirach imoteinu mekor habracha la-avoteinu.
Bless those in need of healing with r'fua sh'leima
the renewal of body, the renewal of spirit.   And let us say -- Amen.

© Debbie Friedman

 El na refa na lahh   אֵל נָא רְפָא נָא לָהּ

❀❀❀❀❀

If you are comfortable doing so, please rise as we lift and dress the Torah

וְזֹאת הַתּוֹרָה אֲשֶׁר שָׂם מֹשֶׁה
לִפְנֵי בְּנֵי יִשְׂרָאֵל עַל פִּי יהוה בְּיַד מֹשֶׁה:

Vezot haTorah asher sam Moshe lifnei benei Yisra-eil al pi Adonai
beyad Moshe.

This is the Torah that Moses placed before the people of Israel, the word of Adonai.

❀❀❀❀❀

The ARK is CLOSED and we are seated.

❀❀❀❀❀

Jonah (abridged)

Chapter 1.1. And the word of Adonai came to Jonah, the son of Amittai, saying,

2. Arise, go to Nineveh, that great city, and cry against it; for their wickedness has come up before me.

3. But Jonah rose to flee to Tarshish from the presence of Adonai, and went down to Jaffa; and he found a ship going to Tarshish;

4. But Adonai sent out a great wind, and there was a mighty tempest in the sea.

5. Then the sailors were afraid, and each one cried to his own god. But Jonah had gone down into the interior of the ship and was fast asleep.

15. So they picked up Jonah, and threw him into the sea; and the sea stopped raging.

Chapter 2.1. And Adonai appointed a great fish to swallow Jonah. And Jonah was in the belly of the fish three days and three nights.

2. Then Jonah prayed to Adonai from the belly of the fish,

11. And Adonai spoke to the fish, and it vomited out Jonah upon the dry land.

Chapter 3.4. And Jonah began to go into the city, a day's journey, and he cried, and said, Another forty days, and Nineveh shall be overthrown.

5. And the people of Nineveh believed God, and proclaimed a fast, and put on sackcloth, from the greatest of them to the least of them.

10. And God saw their doings, that they turned from their evil way; and God repented and he did not do it.

Chapter 4.1. And this displeased Jonah exceedingly, and he was very angry.

2. And he prayed to Adonai, and said, I pray you, O Adonai, is this not what I said when I was still in my country? Therefore I hastened to flee to Tarshish; for I knew that you are a gracious God, and merciful, slow to anger, and of great kindness, and that you repent of the evil.

5. And Jonah went out of the city, sat on the east side of the city, made himself a booth, and sat under it in the shadow, so he could see what would happen.

6. And Adonai appointed a castor oil plant, and made it grow over Jonah, that it might be a shadow over his head. And Jonah was exceedingly glad of the plant.

7. And, when dawn came up the next day, God appointed a worm, and it attacked the plant so that it withered.

8. And it came to pass, when the sun rose, that God appointed a hot east wind; and the sun beat down upon the head of Jonah, so that he fainted, and wished to die, and said, It is better for me to die than to live.

9. And God said to Jonah: Do you do well to be so angry for the plant? And he said: I do well to be so angry, even to death.

10. Then Adonai said, You had concern for the plant, for which you did not labor, nor did you make it grow; which came up in a night, and perished in a night;

11. And should I not spare Nineveh, that great city, where there are more than one hundred and twenty thousand persons who cannot discern between their right hand and their left hand; and also much cattle?

If you are comfortable doing so, please rise as we open the ark for returning the Torah

עֵץ חַיִּים הִיא לַמַּחֲזִיקִים בָּהּ, וְתֹמְכֶיהָ מְאֻשָּׁר. דְּרָכֶיהָ
דַרְכֵי נֹעַם, וְכָל נְתִיבוֹתֶיהָ שָׁלוֹם.

Eitz cha**yim** hi lamachazi**kiym** ba, vetom**che**ha me-u**shar**.
Dera**che**ha dar**chei no**-am, ve**chol** netivo**te**ha sha**lom**.

It is a tree of life to those who hold it fast, and all who cling to it find happiness. Its ways are ways of pleasantness, and all its paths are peace.

הֲשִׁיבֵנוּ יהוה, אֵלֶיךָ וְנָשׁוּבָה, חַדֵּשׁ יָמֵינוּ כְּקֶדֶם.

Hashi**vei**nu Ado**nai**, ei**le**cha vena**shu**va, cha**deish** ya**mei**nu keke**dem**.

Help us to return to You, Adonai; then we will return. Renew our days as in the past.

(If you are comfortable doing so, please remain standing for the Aleinu)

❈❈❈❈❈❈

[The ARK is OPENED or remains OPEN after Torah Service]

If you are comfortable doing so, please remain standing or rise as we open the ark for the Aleinu

ADORATION   עלינו

עָלֵינוּ לְשַׁבֵּחַ לַאֲדוֹן הַכֹּל, לָתֵת גְּדֻלָּה לְיוֹצֵר בְּרֵאשִׁית, שֶׁלֹּא עָשָׂנוּ
עִם גּוֹיֵי הָאֲרָצוֹת, וְלֹא שָׂמָנוּ עִם מִשְׁפְּחוֹת הָאֲדָמָה, שֶׁלֹּא שָׂם
חֶלְקֵנוּ עִמָּהֶם, וְגֹרָלֵנוּ עִם כָּל הָעוֹלָם
וַאֲנַחְנוּ כּוֹרְעִים וּמִשְׁתַּחֲוִים וּמוֹדִים,
לִפְנֵי מֶלֶךְ, מַלְכֵי הַמְּלָכִים, הַקָּדוֹשׁ בָּרוּךְ הוּא.

A**lei**nu lesha**bei**-ach la-a**don** ha**kol**, la**teit** gedu**lah** l'yo**tzeir** b'rei**shiyt**, she**lo**
a**sa**nu iym go**yei** ha-ara**tzot**, ve**lo** sama**na** iym mishpe**chot** ha-ada**mah**, she**lo**
sam chel**kei**nu ima**hem**, v'gora**lei**nu iym kol ha-o**lam**.
V'a**nach**nu kor'**iym** umishtacha**viym** umo**diym**.
Lif**nei Me**lech, mal**chei** hamla**chiym**, haKa**dosh** Baruch Hu.

It is up to us to praise the Source of all, to give due greatness to the One who created at the very beginning, who gave us a purpose among the nations of the earth, sending us among the families of the earth, giving us a Divine assignment, working with all of the world.

Therefore, we bend our knees, bow, approach and give thanks before the Ultimate Sovereign, The Holy One, the Source of Blessing.

❈❈❈❈❈❈

If you are more comfortable sitting, please do so at this time or at any time.

❈❈❈❈❈❈

Let us adore the ever living God, and render praise unto You,
who spread out the heavens and established the earth,
whose glory is revealed in the heavens above, and whose greatness is manifest
throughout the world. You are our God, there is none else.
We bow the head in reverence and worship
HaKadosh Baruch Hu, the Holy One, Praised be God.
Va-anachnu koriym umishtachaviym umodiym lifnei Melech malchei hamlachiym,
HaKadosh Baruch Hu, the Holy One, Praised be God. Amen.

(Ark is closed -- Please be seated)

May the time not be distant, O God, when Your name will be worshipped in all
the earth, when unbelief will disappear and error be no more.

Fervently we pray that the day may come when all will turn to You in love, when
corruption and evil will give way to integrity and goodness, when superstition will no
longer enslave the mind, nor idolatry blind the eye, when all who dwell on earth will
know that You alone are God. O may all, created in Your image, become one in spirit and
one in friendship, forever united in Your service. Then will Your rule be established on
earth, and the word of Your prophet fulfilled: the Eternal God will reign for ever and
ever.

And then both men and women will be gentle,
And then both women and men will be strong,
And then all will be so varied, rich and free,
And then everywhere will be called Eden once again.

Judy Chicago (adapted)

וְנֶאֱמַר, וְהָיָה יהוה לְמֶלֶךְ עַל כָּל הָאָרֶץ, בַּיּוֹם הַהוּא יִהְיֶה יהוה
אֶחָד, וּשְׁמוֹ אֶחָד:

V'ne-e**mar**, v'ha**ya** Adonai l'**me**lech al kol ha-**aretz**, ba**yom** hahu yiye Adonai
e**chad**, ush'**mo** e**chad**.

On that day, O God, You will be One and Your Name will be One.

יזכר **Remembering**

יְהוָה, יְהוָה, אֵל רַחוּם וְחַנּוּן, אֶרֶךְ אַפַּיִם, וְרַב חֶסֶד וֶאֱמֶת: נֹצֵר חֶסֶד לָאֲלָפִים, נֹשֵׂא עָוֹן וָפֶשַׁע וְחַטָּאָה, וְנַקֵּה:

Adonai Ado**nai** Eil ra**chum** vecha**nun**, **erech** a**pay**im ve**rav che**sed ve-e**met**,
no**tzeir che**sed la-ala**fiym**, no**sei** a**von** va**fe**sha vechata-**ah** vena**kei**.

Adonai, Adonai, God of compassion and grace, slow to anger and abounding with mercy and truth.
You grant mercy to the thousands, lifting shame and inequity and sin; You are cleansing.

✿ ✿ ✿ ✿ ✿ ✿

Four times a year we are invited by our tradition
to remember those we love who have passed on.
These times are Yom Kippur, the end of Passover, Shavuot
and the end of Succot/Shmini Atzeret.
> *These are times when our tradition teaches that the Gates of Prayer*
> *are particularly open and we can draw most powerfully on those we remember*
> *and seek healing of the wounds from that separation.*

In the safety of our loving community,
we can expose these wounds and give them a chance to breathe and to heal.
Healing does not mean that we love the departed souls any less,
for love shared will never die.
> *Rather it honors their memory*
> *and shifts that memory from one of pain and hurt to one of blessing and joy*
> *of having had that bond, that connection, in the first place.*
> *If we did not love them and connect to them at a soul level,*
> *we would not feel hurt in our souls for their passing from our daily routines.*

Healing does not mean forgetting, rather it means remembering,
remembering with love and joy.
Dear One, help us to move from the place of pain to the place of love,
from the place of sorrow to the place of living,
from the hurt of loss to the joy of remembering.
> *Jewish tradition teaches us that between the world of the living*
> *and the world of the dead there is a window and not a wall.*

This has stood in contrast to our culture of scientific materialism
which teaches that dead is dead,
and after death, the channels of communication between us
and our loved ones who have died are forever ended - a brick wall!

To Life! High Holy Day Prayer Book

מחזור לחיים

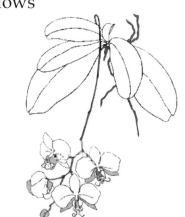

The rituals of *Shiva*, *Kaddish*, *Yahrzeit* and *Yizkor* open windows
to the unseen worlds of the dead.
Yizkor creates a sacred space and time
wherein we can open our hearts and minds
to the possibility of a genuine inter-connection
with beloved family members and friends
who have left behind the world of the living.
Yizkor is a window.
Prepare to open that window as...
We remember them

❀ ❀ ❀ ❀ ❀

23rd Psalm, a Psalm of David

א מִזְמוֹר לְדָוִד יהוה רֹעִי לֹא אֶחְסָר:

Mizmor L'Da**vid**: Ado**nai ro**-i lo ech**sar**

A Psalm of David. Adonai is my shepherd; I will not be lacking.

ב בִּנְאוֹת דֶּשֶׁא יַרְבִּיצֵנִי עַל־מֵי מְנֻחוֹת יְנַהֲלֵנִי:

Bin'**ot de**she yarbiy**tzei**ni al mei menu**chot** y'naha**lei**ni.

God causes me to lie down [where my soul can catch its breath] in green pastures; besides the calming waters.

ג נַפְשִׁי יְשׁוֹבֵב יַנְחֵנִי בְמַעְגְּלֵי־צֶדֶק לְמַעַן שְׁמוֹ:

Naf**shi** yesho**veiv** yan**chei**niy vema'**glei tze**dek l'**ma**-an she**mo**.

God restores my soul; leading me in the ways of living righteousness for that is God's essence.

ד גַּם כִּי־אֵלֵךְ בְּגֵיא צַלְמָוֶת לֹא־אִירָא רָע כִּי־אַתָּה עִמָּדִי

Gam ki ei**leich** be**gei** tzal**ma**vet lo iy**ra** ra ki **A**ta ima**diy**.

Even though I find myself walking through the depths of the valley, feeling the very shadow of death, I will not fear evil; for you are with me;

שִׁבְטְךָ וּמִשְׁעַנְתֶּךָ הֵמָּה יְנַחֲמֻנִי:

Shivte**cha** umish'an**te**cha **hei**ma yenacha**mu**niy.

Your rod and your staff guide and comfort me.

ה תַּעֲרֹךְ לְפָנַי שֻׁלְחָן נֶגֶד צֹרְרָי דִּשַּׁנְתָּ בַשֶּׁמֶן רֹאשִׁי כּוֹסִי רְוָיָה:

Ta-aroch lefa**nai** shul**chan ne**ged tzore**rai** di**shan**ta vashe**men** ro**shi** co**si** re**va**ya.

You arrange a table before me, even in the presence of my detractors; you anoint my head with oil; my cup runs over.

וּ אַךְ טוֹב וָחֶסֶד יִרְדְּפוּנִי כָּל־יְמֵי חַיָּי

Ach tov va**che**sed yir'de**fu**niy kol ye**mei** cha**yai**

Surely goodness and loving kindness will follow me all the days of my life;

וְשַׁבְתִּי בְּבֵית־יהוה לְאֹרֶךְ יָמִים:

Veshav**tiy** be**veit** Ado**nai** l'**orech** ya**miym**

and I will live with Adonai's presence in the house of my soul forever.

❦❦❦❦❦ ❦❦❦❦❦

We remember them

At the rising of the sun and at its going down, we remember them.
At the blowing of the wind and in the chill of winter, we remember them.
   At the opening of the buds and in the rebirth of spring, we remember them.
   At the blueness of the skies and in the warmth of summer, we remember them.

At the rustling of the leaves and in the beauty of autumn, we remember them.
At the beginning of the year and when it ends, we remember them.
   As long as we live, they too will live:
   for they are now a part of us, as we remember them.

When we are weary and in need of strength,   we remember them.
When we are lost and sick at heart, we remember them.
   When we have joy we crave to share, we remember them.
   When we have decisions that are difficult to make, we remember them.

When we have achievements that are based on theirs, we remember them.
When we have achievements that would make them proud, we remember them.
   As long as we live, they too will live;
   for they are now a part of us, as we remember them.

❦❦❦❦❦ ❦❦❦❦❦

Eli, Eli   אֵלִי, אֵלִי

אֵלִי, אֵלִי שֶׁלֹּא יִגָּמֵר לְעוֹלָם:
הַחוֹל וְהַיָּם, רִשְׁרוּשׁ שֶׁל הַמַּיִם,
בְּרַק הַשָּׁמַיִם, תְּפִלַּת הָאָדָם.

Eli, Eli, Shelo yiga**meir** le-o**lam:**
Hachol veha**yam**, rish**rush** shel ha**ma**yim,
be**rak** hasha**ma**yim, tefi**lat** ha-a**dam.**
Oh God, my God, I pray that these things never end:
the sand and the sea, the rush of the waters,
the crash of the heavens, the prayer of the heart
© Hannah Senesh

❦❦❦❦❦ ❦❦❦❦❦

❀❀❀❀❀ ❀❀❀❀❀

Life is like a candle's flame.

Life is like a candle's flame.
It must have just the right amount of air and wick and wax to burn brightly.

If there is no air, there can be no flame.
If there is too much air, it will burn out quickly.

At any time, it is easily snuffed out.
It is beautiful while it burns brightly before us.

It must work together with other parts of its environment
to have its full beauty be appreciated.

If it gets out of control, the results can be pure horror or wickedness
and people may be harmed by it.
Most of the time, however, the flame give us light, comfort and joy.

Each candle's flame does this, each one is special when we look at it.
The shape and appearance of the flame
changes with every moment as we look at it, it is never static.

A single candle flame can pierce the darkest space.
With the light of a single candle, the dark place is no longer completely dark.
The light of a single candle can guide us through the darkness.

One candle's flame can light another candle
and both will shine brightly without diminishing the other.
One candle flame can light many candles, turning their potential into reality.

The light from a single candle can spread throughout the world,
each candle flame lighting another's,
each burning with their own special glow and in their own unique way.

They can join together and raise a flame
that is larger than the sum of the parts
and they can separate without either losing its flame.

The flame of the candle is like our souls.
Rabbi Shafir Lobb

❀❀❀❀❀ ❀❀❀❀❀

⊱⊰

YIZKOR RITUAL

⊱⊰

❀❀❀❀❀ ❀❀❀❀❀

Yom Kippur

For a male

יִזְכֹּר אֱלֹהִים נִשְׁמַת יַקִירִי _ בֶּן _ שֶׁהָלַךְ לְעוֹלָמוֹ, בַּעֲבוּר שֶׁבְּלִי נֶדֶר אֶתֵּן צְדָקָה בַּעֲדוֹ. בִּשְׂכַר נַפְשׁוֹ צְרוּרָה בִּצְרוֹר הַחַיִּים עִם נִשְׁמוֹת אַבְרָהָם יִצְחָק וְיַעֲקֹב, שָׂרָה רִבְקָה רָחֵל וְלֵאָה, וְעִם שְׁאָר צַדִּיקִים וְצִדְקָנִיּוֹת שֶׁבְּגַן עֵדֶן, וְנֹאמַר אָמֵן.

Yiz**kor** Elo**hiym** nish**mat** yaki**ri** _____ ben _____ sheha**lach** le-ola**mo**, ba-a**vur** she**bli ne**der e**tein** tzeda**kah** ba-a**do**. Bis**char** naf**sho** tzeru**ra** bitz**ror** hachay**yim** im nish**mot** Avra**ham** Yitz**chak** veYa-a**kov** Sa**ra** Riv**ka** Ra**cheil** veLe-**ah**, ve-**im** she-**ar** tzadiy**kiym** vetzidkani**yot** shebe**Gan Ei**den, veno**mar** a**mein**.

May the memory of my dear _____ son of _____, who returned to You, the Source of All, be sanctified in me. May I be led to acts of Tzedakah in his memory, for the sake of blessing. Dear Holy One, may his Soul be bound up with those of our ancestors, Abraham, Isaac, Jacob, Sarah, Rebeccah, Rachel and Leah and with those pious Souls that are in Gan Eden. And let us say, Amen.

For a female

יִזְכֹּר אֱלֹהִים נִשְׁמַת יַקִירָתִי _ בַּת _ שֶׁהָלְכָה לְעוֹלָמָהּ, בַּעֲבוּר שֶׁבְּלִי נֶדֶר אֶתֵּן צְדָקָה בַּעֲדָהּ. בִּשְׂכַר נַפְשָׁהּ צְרוּרָה בִּצְרוֹר הַחַיִּים עִם נִשְׁמוֹת אַבְרָהָם יִצְחָק וְיַעֲקֹב, שָׂרָה רִבְקָה רָחֵל וְלֵאָה, וְעִם שְׁאָר צַדִּיקִים וְצִדְקָנִיּוֹת שֶׁבְּגַן עֵדֶן, וְנֹאמַר אָמֵן.

Yiz**kor** Elo**hiym** nish**mat** yaki**rati** _____ bat _____ sheha**lcha** le-ola**mahh**, ba-a**vur** she**bli ne**der e**tein** tzeda**kah** ba-a**dahh**. Bis**char** naf**shahh** tzeru**ra** bitz**ror** hachay**yim** im nish**mot** Avra**ham** Yitz**chak** veYa-a**kov** Sa**ra** Riv**ka** Ra**cheil** veLe-**ah**, ve-**im** she-**ar** tzadiy**kiym** vetzidkani**yot** shebe**Gan Ei**den, veno**mar** a**mein**.

May the memory of my dear _____ daughter of _____, who returned to You, the Source of All, be sanctified in me. May I be led to acts of Tzedakah in her memory, for the sake of blessing. Dear Holy One, may her Soul be bound up with those of our ancestors, Abraham, Isaac, Jacob, Sarah, Rebeccah, Rachel and Leah and with those pious Souls that are in Gan Eden. And let us say, Amen.

God of Compassion אל מלא

אֵל מָלֵא רַחֲמִים שׁוֹכֵן בַּמְּרוֹמִים. הַמְצֵא מְנוּחָה נְכוֹנָה עַל כַּנְפֵי
הַשְּׁכִינָה. בְּמַעֲלוֹת קְדוֹשִׁים וּטְהוֹרִים כְּזֹהַר הָרָקִיעַ מַזְהִירִים אֶת
נִשְׁמַת כָּל אֵלֶה שֶׁהָלַךְ לְעוֹלָמָם בַּעֲבוּר שֶׁבְּלִי נֶדֶר אֶתֵּן צְדָקָה בְּעַד
הַזְכָּרַת נִשְׁמָתָם, בְּגַן עֵדֶן תְּהֵא מְנוּחָתָם. לָכֵן בַּעַל הָרַחֲמִים יַסְתִּירֵהוּ
בְּסֵתֶר כְּנָפָיו לְעוֹלָמִים. וְיִצְרוֹר בִּצְרוֹר הַחַיִּים אֶת נִשְׁמָתָם. יְהֹוָה הוּא
נַחֲלָתָם: וְיָנוּחַ בְּשָׁלוֹם עַל מִשְׁכָּבָם. וְנֹאמַר אָמֵן:

El malei rachamiym shochein bamromiym. Hamtzei menuchah nechonah tachat kanfei haShechinah. Bema-alot kedushiym ut-horiym kezohar harakiyah mazhiriym et nishmat kol eileh shehalach le-olamam, Ba-avur shebli neder, etein tzedakah be-ad hazkarat nishmatam. BeGan Eiden tehei menuchatam. Lachein ba-al harachamiym yastireihu beseiter kenafav le-olamiym. Veyitzror bitzror hachayim et nishmatam. Adonai Hu nachalatam. V'tanu-ach beshalom al mishkavam. Venomar Amein.

O compassionate God, who dwells in the high places, grant complete repose to these souls who have gone to Your realm. May it be under the wings of the Shechina in the heavens, where this holy and pure soul, that sparkles as the bright lights of the firmament, can rest. For the sake of these souls, we pledge to give tzedaka for the memory of these souls. May the Garden of Eden be their resting place. May their souls be treasured and protected under Your wings to all the realms. May these souls be gathered and bound with the other treasured and immortal souls for eternal life. Adonai, may You treasure them and may they rest in peace. And let us say, Amen.

קדיש יתום

Mourner's Kaddish

We now ask those of you who are in mourning or who are observing the *Yahrzeit* of a loved one to stand and share their names with us.... Let us support you through the first paragraph and then rise with you.   In this way we can link our memories with yours in the hope that we will thus draw strength and comfort from each other. Together we praise God's name.   (English translation on pages 47 & 48)

יִתְגַּדַּל וְיִתְקַדַּשׁ שְׁמֵהּ רַבָּא. בְּעָלְמָא דִּי בְרָא כִרְעוּתֵיהּ, וְיַמְלִיךְ מַלְכוּתֵיהּ בְּחַיֵּיכוֹן וּבְיוֹמֵיכוֹן וּבְחַיֵּי דְכָל בֵּית יִשְׂרָאֵל. בַּעֲגָלָא וּבִזְמַן קָרִיב וְאִמְרוּ אָמֵן:

Yitga**dal** v'yitka**dash** shi**mei** ra**ba** b'al**ma** di v'ra chiru**tei**, v'yam**lich** malchu**tei** b'chayei**chon** uv'yomei**chon** uv'cha**yei** d'chol beit Yisra-**eil**, ba-aga**la**, ba-aga**la**, uviz**man** ka**riv**, v'im'ru: **A**mein.

יְהֵא שְׁמֵהּ רַבָּא מְבָרַךְ לְעָלַם וּלְעָלְמֵי עָלְמַיָּא:

Ye**hei** sh'mei **ra**ba m'va**rach** l'a**lam** ul'al**mei** alma**ya**.

יִתְבָּרַךְ וְיִשְׁתַּבַּח וְיִתְפָּאַר וְיִתְרוֹמַם וְיִתְנַשֵּׂא וְיִתְהַדָּר וְיִתְעַלֶּה וְיִתְהַלָּל שְׁמֵהּ דְּקֻדְשָׁא בְּרִיךְ הוּא לְעֵלָּא לְעֵלָּא מִכָּל בִּרְכָתָא וְשִׁירָתָא תֻּשְׁבְּחָתָא וְנֶחֱמָתָא, דַּאֲמִירָן בְּעָלְמָא, וְאִמְרוּ אָמֵן:

Yitba**rach**, v'yishta**bach**, v'yitpa-**ar**, v'yitro**mam**, v'yitna**sei**, v'yit-ha**dar**, v'yit-a**leh**, v'yit-ha**lal** sh'mei d'kud**sha**, brich hu. L'**ei**la l'**ei**la mi**kol** bircha**ta** v'shira**ta**, tushb'cha**ta** v'nechema**ta** da-ami**ran** b'al**ma**, v'im'ru: Amein.

יְהֵא שְׁלָמָא רַבָּא מִן שְׁמַיָּא, וְחַיִּים עָלֵינוּ וְעַל כָּל יִשְׂרָאֵל וְאִמְרוּ אָמֵן.

Y'**hei** sh'**la**ma **ra**ba min sh'ma**ya**, v'cha**yim** alei**nu** v'**al** kol Yisra-**eil**, v'imru: a**mein**.

עֹשֶׂה שָׁלוֹם בִּמְרוֹמָיו הוּא יַעֲשֶׂה שָׁלוֹם עָלֵינוּ וְעַל כָּל יִשְׂרָאֵל, (וְעַל כָּל יוֹשְׁבֵי תֵבֵל,) וְאִמְרוּ אָמֵן:

Oseh sha**lom** bimro**mav**, hu ya-a**seh** sha**lom** alei**nu**, v'**al** kol Yisra-**eil**, (v'**al** kol yosh**vei** tey**veil**,) v'imru: a**mein**.

May the Source of peace send peace to all who mourn and comfort to all who are bereaved in our midst, and let us say, Amen.

Neila is the closing of the gates that happens each night at sunset
Today is a special day and we can imagine the sun is about to set.

> *And so the gates that are about to close are not those of the city*
> *But of our hearts and souls.*

Soon we will return from this time spent in prayer, meditation and thought.
A time of focus and Soul work and deep honesty with Self and God,
the Source of all Life.

> *We have worked at pealing away the indifference,*
> *the vestiges of ego and self-investment*
> *Hoping to bring more ownership and acceptance*
> *of our own actions and responsibilities*

Dear Source of All Life, let us turn to you and find the trust
that we have wanted to place in You and in our own Self.
Give us the strength and the courage
to allow you to guide us through the gates of our own dark valleys.

> *O Compassionate one, carry us through that gate*
> *and help us find the courage and the strength*
> *to let You take us inside that last Gate of Self.*

Do we need to change?

Perhaps, how can we know?

Nothing ever stays the same, everything changes.

> *Winds change direction, rivers change course.*
> *Clouds change shape, caterpillars change form.*
> *No thing or person ever stays the same.*

Everyone changes.

> *One cell becomes two; two become four.*
> *What we were and what we are*
> *Give way to what we will become.*
> *And there is no choice,*

Except for who we choose to become.
The question is not will we change, but how will we change.

> *Today is a day for change.*
> *Today is a day for growth.*
> *We are here to change*
> *We are here to grow.*

שְׁמַע יִשְׂרָאֵל, יהוה אֱלֹהֵינוּ, יהוה אֶחָד:

Shema Yisra**eil**, Ado**nai** Elo**hei**nu, Ado**nai** E**chad**.

Listen Israel, Adonai is our God, Adonai is One.

בָּרוּךְ שֵׁם כְּבוֹד מַלְכוּתוֹ לְעוֹלָם וָעֶד:(3)

Baruch Sheim ke**vod**, malechu**to**, le-o**lam** Va-**ed**.

A Source of Blessing is God's Holy Name, God's sovereignty endures throughout time and space.

יהוה הוּא הָאֱלֹהִים (7)

Ado**nai** Hu haElo**hiym**.

Adonai is God.

תְּקִיעָה גְדוֹלָה!!

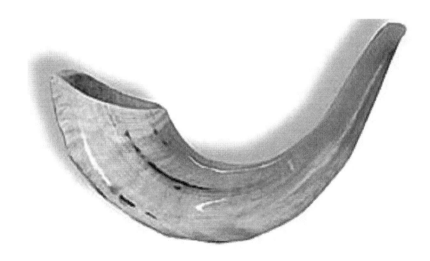

Rabbi Shafir Lobb is currently the rabbi at Congregation Kol Simchah in Tucson, Arizona. She received *smicha*, ordination, through the ALEPH Rabbinical Program. She has served as a chaplain with VNA Hospice in Cleveland Ohio and with Akron General Medical Center in Akron, Ohio. She is currently the President of the Tucson Board of Rabbis and serves on various Boards of Directors, including the Jewish Federation of Southern Arizona, the Jewish History Museum, Jewish Family and Children's Service and the Jewish Community Relations Council. She has compiled and edited many *Siddurim* (Prayer Books) and *Machzorim* (High Holy Day Prayer Books), including special congregational editions. Please check out her web site: www.rabbishafirlobb.com

Made in the USA
San Bernardino, CA
27 August 2015